Spice'n'Easy

by

Hajra Makda

Dedication

*This book is dedicated to the memories of those whom not a day goes by without their rememberance.
my late father Haji Ahmed Seedat my late mother Hajani Fatima Seedat and
my late sister Hajani Hawa Patel (May the Almighty rest their souls in peace.)*

*Growing up in a busy family environment where meals were always considered the favorite subject, it was only natural that at an early age my passion for food was emerging.
My parents took great pride in what was served at the table, with father at the head and mother on his right, followed by two brothers and five sisters, ending with myself at the left of my father.
At the end of a busy day the family meal was treated with a certain degree of seriousness, reverence and respect. What is pleasing is that this enthusiasm we shared as a family has even filtered down to the next generation. In my household, I am pleased to say, my two sons, Rizwaan & Junaid have inherited those streaks too! I have already seen the signs emerging as they sometimes enthusiastically offer their advice, opinion and help when they so delightfully invade my territory in the kitchen.
Even today my late parents and sister are remembered for their excellent taste of good food, of course among other remarkable things, and I listen with great pride. For they always taught us that food is a bounty from the Almighty and that you should appreciate all good things in life, and make the most of every precious moment.*

Acknowledgements

*First and foremost I would like to express my sincere gratitude and appreciation to my husband and my two sons, Rizwaan and Junaid, who have provided me with endless hours of moral support and encouragement.
I would also like to extend my gratitude to each and everyone who offered me their valued comments, criticism, advice and help in numerous ways. It would be practically impossible to mention each one of you individually but I am sure that without all of you this ambition of mine would not have been possible. My sincere thanks to one and all.*

ISBN 0 9535617 0 4

Web address: **www.sweetnspicy.com**

Published in the UK, by Tropic Publications.
Printed in the UK by VIP Print, Heathfield.

A catalogue record of this book is available from the British Library.

In this book quantities are given in Metric and Imperial measures. Exact conversions from one measure to another does not usually give very convenient working quantities, so the metric measurements have been rounded off to the nearest units.

Book Design
Dipak Chauhan

Photography
Kiran Patel
Robin Allcock
Helen McCann

Illustrations
Samantha O'Brien
Caroline Murphy

Project Editor
Hajra Makda

Gratitude cannot be measured in ounces
or grams but only in silent prayer.
© Hajra Makda

contents

Contents

About the Author

Hajra Makda demonstrates and teaches the art of baking and cooking at various National and International venues.
She works closely with various food companies as a freelance consultant advising on recipe development and packaging design.
Hajra contributes and submits regular articles to various publications at home and abroad and has made several television appearances.
Hajra is currently working on her third book in this series.
She has recently launched her own choice selection of starters, savouries, chutneys & pickles, under the HAJRA'S brand. For further information of HAJRA'S products contact the publisher at the address below.

About Spice 'n' Easy

Spice 'n' Easy contains a mix of over 130 recipes, 16 full colour photographs and appropriate illustrations. Some traditional others adapted to suit the palates across generations. Ranging from starters to main meals and desserts.

The dishes are suitable for everyday or entertaining purposes and are written in the most simplest form, making them easy to understand and to follow.

The instant recipes and masalas are for those days when you are simply pushing for time. But you can be assured that you will be able to produce and serve a nutritional and satisfying meal with maximum flavour and visual appeal in the shortest possible time.

What makes this book even more special, is that it contains extra nutritional information, hints and tips and ideas for serving.

The International section provides a hint of what can be achieved, and with a little creativity and enthusiasm you will surprise yourself at your own capabilities. Many include geographical details of the country they originated from. Easy to undrstand and even easier to creat. Try them and see!

About Sweet 'n' Easy

Second in the series of 'EASY' books by Hajra Makda.
Sweet 'n' Easy contains over 130 irresistible recipes and mouth watering photographs for cakes, biscuits and sumptuous desserts.

The Author shares a selection of outrageously delicious recipes, handed down in the family through generations. To this superb collection she has added her own adaptations and creativity, merging ideas and ingredients from other countries and cultures that impressed her during her travels.

Discover a whole new attitude to baking and making with this amazing mix of mystical Eastern and mouth watering Western concoctions.
Sample the Passion Fruit Biscuits, Turkish Delight, Olive Oil Cake from the Mediterranean or the Date Helawi from the Middle East and many more.

Each traditional and modern, simple yet elaborate, sweet temptation has been carefully selected, tried, tested and tasted. You'll be spoilt for choice!

PRICE £ 8.99 ISBN 0 9535617 1 2
Published in the UK by Tropic Publications, PO Box 5786, Leicester, LE5 5WL, UK.
For product information write to Tropic Publications.

The aim of this book was to provide simple yet traditional recipes and to show you that Indian cookery is not as difficult as you may think.
I wanted to write a book that was accessible to people of all ages, to reach across generations, cultures and nationality, regardless of race and religion.
I have tried to offer a balanced selection of dishes which you could adopt for everyday consumption and also for entertaining purposes.
In this world of hectic lifestyles there simply has to be more creativity and panache. Use your common sense, your talent. Use the measurements and temperatures as a guide only, and above all do not abandon your judgement and initiative. These are just simple recipes to tempt you into learning the culinary art, to be confident when receiving guests and to be adventurous with cooking methods and dishes other then your own.
The International section is for you to gain an insight into what can be achieved. Use your imagination and skills, adapt the recipe to your taste. Take an interest in what people from other cultures and countries eat and how they cook. If you look into a spice tin of someone from another culture you will be surprised to find the contents very similar to your own.
When on vacation try and find out how certain foods are prepared and presented. You will be surprised at the sheer pleasure they take in sharing the recipes.
Certain spices and powders are universally recognised. If they are not familiar ask and learn about them. There is a wealth of knowledge to be gained, but only if you ask.
The secret of good cooking lies in a well stocked pantry. It is from here that the Indian cook can create culinary masterpieces.
Though all the spices are carefully blended to enhance a particular dish, you must appreciate that cooking is an art, an art to be enjoyed. If you are not familiar with certain spices I would advise that you read the introduction and study the spices used to give a deeper insight.
Learn about the medicinal benefits that can be derived. Familiarise yourself with the techniques.
Be adventurous, experiment, don't worry if the first time it doesn't turn out as it should, never mind, try again, never give up. There are no basic rules for cookery, nothing has to be rigidly stuck to.
However, having said this I always stress the importance of being fair to the author of any cookery book. You can make your own additions and subtractions to suit your individual taste.
It would be practically impossible to say that your dishes will turn out exactly the same as mine. The garlic you use may be young or old. The mango may not be as sweet or ripe. The large lemon has very little juice, the chilli not as hot or red. Nature has its own way. What I am trying to say is allow for these small but important things.
And always try and buy the freshest produce as this will greatly enhance the flavour of any dish.
But remember it is that personal touch, simply of having the knack of turning out a dish in no time with little effort and remarkable taste and appearance. That will be your personal signature. And that is what will be remembered.
Adjust the seasoning as you go along and learn to trust in yourself.
Everybody can be a good cook, each of us have a talent and flair.
Although I was inspired by many well known names you yourself will have such a talent, and you probably don't have to search very far for it too.
Try and eat regular and wholesome meals.
Be careful with the level of fats and ghee used. There is no need for a meat or vegetables to be swimming in fat or oils. You can reduce the fat content of the of recipes effectively without sacrificing the aroma and taste of these exotic recipes.
Adapt a healthy attitude.
Many people are only accustomed to eating different foods in restaurants. I strongly believe that you cannot beat good home cooking. The immense pleasure at the table when the guest shows his or her appreciation should not be missed.
In my attempt to divert your attention away from fast foods and such I have tried to make the recipes as simple and uncomplicated as possible. Allow yourself that little indulgence in exploring other culinary delights.
I sincerely hope that my enthusiasm will in time rub off onto the readers and that I have managed to inspire you to grab that apron and spice tin, step into your kitchen and truly explore your capabilities and creative talents.
Happy eating!

هاجرة ماكدا

Hajra Makda

hints & tips

When storing green chillies remove the stems.
This will help the chillies retain their freshness for a longer period.

When coconut milk has been kept overnight in the fridge it will form a white layer over the top, use this layer as fat when cooking, it is much healthier.

To preserve coriander leaves, keep in a glass jar in the fridge. They will retain their freshness for longer without discolouring.

Instead of adding yoghurt to chutney try adding lime juice, the chutney will have a sharper taste and will retain its colour as well as freshness.

To keep garlic skins from sticking to your hands when skinning, soak in cold water for an hour. This will enable the skins to slip off more easily.

Ginger can be skinned much easier when soaked in cold water and scraped with a knife.

Don't worry if your curry has become salty add potato cubes which will take the saltiness away and remove before serving.

If you suffer from insomnia eat a teaspoon of cumin powder mixed with the pulp of a ripe banana and this will induce peaceful sleep at night.

Add ½ tsp of sugar cane juice to old and dried pickles it will taste as delicious as freshly made pickles.

When cooking rice add two drops of lemon juice the rice will remain fluffy and not stick together.

Add 2-3 tablespoons of home made paneer or milk with the water to wheat flour. You will get a soft, smooth nutritious dough for chappati and paratha.

Do not add raw oil to pickles boil the oil until just smokey, cook and then top up the jar, this will prevent the formation of fungus.

Grinding a small quantity of cardammon is sometimes difficult. Instead add a small quantity of sugar, not only will it be easier it will also impart a better flavour.

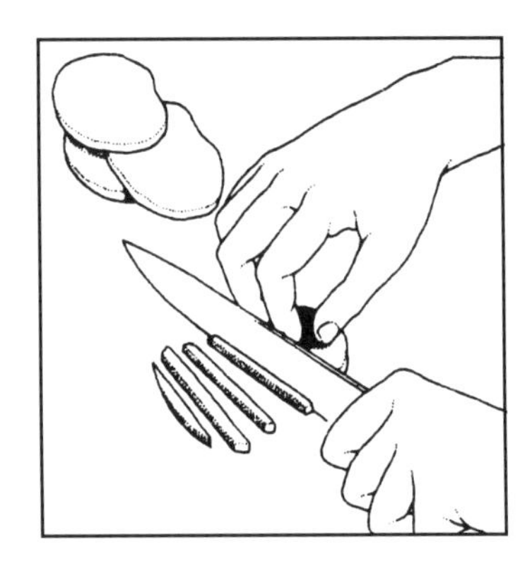

Cauliflower will retain its natural colour while cooking if you add a teaspoon of lemon juice to it.

When cooking leafy vegetables like spinach, it is recommended to add the salt at the end when almost cooked. This is to avoid the dish becoming salty as the quantity reduces as it cooks.

For a quick salad dressing, blend a cup of curd with a little lime juice and seasoning, and pour over the salad.

Basmati Rice

Of all the different species of rice, basmati is by far the best and well worth a little extra expense. It has fine long grains with a wonderful aroma and a distinctive flavour which makes even plain rice a treat. Basmati cooks relatively quickly and providing it has been washed to remove all the starch the grains will be full and separate.

Coconut

Unless a recipe specifies desiccated coconut it is better to use fresh coconut which may easily be grated in a blender or food processor. Most recipes only require a small amount but since grated coconut freezes well and defrosts quickly it's worth storing for future use.

Coconut Milk

Tinned coconut milk is usually available from grocers but make sure you buy the unsweetened variety. Creamed coconut is more easily available and may also be used to make coconut milk. Simply put 5 level tablespoons in a bowl and slowly add / pint of hot water. Mix thoroughly. It will give you about 8 fl oz of coconut milk.

Flour

All the flours mentioned in this book are available from most Asian supermarkets.

Bajra Flour

Bajra flour is millet flour, a highly nutritious cereal ideal for those following a low-fibre, gluten-free diet. In addition for use in making rotla and millet bread a small amount mixed into pizza dough makes a lovely crispy base.

Barley Flour

To make both Indian style bread and a close-textured, delicately flavoured leavened bread which stays fresh for several days. This type of bread is ideal for those whose diet does not allow them to eat wheat products.

Cornmeal

Cornmeal is milled in both coarse and fine grain from yellow maize where the germ and oil have been removed. Do not confuse cornmeal with cornflour (cornstarch) which is principally a thickening agent.

Dahi Vada Flour

Ground rice and pulses which form the principal ingredient in the delicious batter balls of the same name.

Dhosa Flour

A special flour ground from rice and urad dahl used to make the delicious, crisp pancake-dhosas of Southern India.

Gram Flour (Chick Pea Flour)

Gram flour is a very finely ground pale blond flour made from kale chana, a variety of chick peas, and is always used in Indian cuisine when cooking bhajias and pakoras as well as in some sweets. But don't keep it just for Indian cuisine; substitute it for wheat flour in crumbles, cakes and even short-crust pastry although it will be difficult to roll out) for a richer flavour, like soya flour and rice flour gram flour is suitable for those following a gluten-free diet.

Juwar Flour

Juwar flour is milled from a form of millet known as sorgum. Very easily digested it is suitable for rotla.

Ondhwa Flour

Ondhwa flour is milled from rice and gram and is used in making handvo, a speciality of Gujarat.

Rice Flour

Has the same texture as cornflour but is gluten free. Made from ground white rice.

Laapsi

Crushed wheat. Made into a sweet dish.

Mattar Ata

Flour made from peas and used for making savouries.

Semolina

Semolina is available in both fine and coarse ground qualities. As well as being used in milk puddings semolina is used to make gnocchi and to give a gritty texture to some cakes and biscuits. It is also an excellent substitute for flour when coating food prior to frying, the results are crisper.

White Maize Flour

Ground from the original white maize this flour has a wonderful aroma and is used extensively in African cookery.

Whole WheatFlour Chapatti Flour

Whole wheat flours vary considerably although they should always be milled from the whole grain of wheat. 'Strength' of the flour that is the gluten content which helps baked food to rise and hold its shape, depends principally on where the wheat is grown. This flour will make the best chappatti bread you have ever tasted.

Ghee

Ghee is simply butter which has been clarified to remove all the milk solids so that you may even deep fry in it. If you cannot buy ready made ghee make your own with 225g - 8oz of the best unsalted butter you can. Put it in a small, heavy pan and allow to melt over a low Heat. Simmer it very gently for about 45 minutes without stirring, until the milk solids turn brown and cling to the sides of the pan or all to the bottom (do not allow the butter itself to brown). Finally strain the ghee through a few layers of cheesecloth. Homemade ghee is best stored covered in the refrigerator.

Oil

Flavoursome oils are not generally used in Indian cuisine, with the exception of specialities such as sesame, mustard or olive oil which you may occasionally find specified in recipes. Ghee is a more traditional cooking medium than oil but wherever possible all the recipes in this book specify oil for healthier eating. Any lightly flavoured vegetable oil will do, such as groundnut, corn oil, sunflower seed or safflower oil.

Pawa

Pawa is a special type of flat rice. In addition to the recipe mentioned in this book it makes a delicious snack when deep fried and mixed with spices.

Poppadoms

Poppadoms, sometimes called papads, are the savoury wafer made from urad flour which are served with every Indian meal. To make them requires years of practice and unlimited sunshine so it is advisable to admit defeat and buy them ready-made. At their best poppadoms are paper-thin and incredibly crispy and may be cooked in a few seconds under a very hot grill or fried.

Quorn or Soya

Quorn or soya meat can be substituted in recipes which include meat.

Poultry

The skin has been removed from all the poultry recipes used in this book.

Pulses

Pulses - dried peas, beans and lentils - are high in protein so it is not surprising that they are used so extensively in Indian cooking where more than 75% of the population are vegetarian. They are also a good source of iron, phosphorus and the B vitamins. They have the lowest at content of any of the protein foods yet of all foods they offer the richest sources of fibre. But, more important for those who love food, cooked properly, particularly in combination with various spices, they are also absolutely delicious.

Aduki Beans

A small roundish red-brown coloured bean with a sweet, strong, nutty flavour.

Black Eye Beans

Black eye beans are fairly small, kidney shaped and cream-coloured with a black spot or eye. They are one of the quicker cooking pulses with a savoury flavour and may be used as a substitute for haricot or butter beans.

Brown Lentils (Masoor)

The whole lentil from which masoor dhal or red split lentils are obtained.

Butter Beans

A large, flat kidney shaped bean with a creamy white colour.

Chana Dhal

Like yellow split peas but smaller in size and sweeter.

Chick Peas

Popular in Middle Eastern and Mediterranean cookery chick peas are round in shape and pale golden brown in colour. When cooked they retain their shape. The Indian name for chick peas is Chana.

Chora Dhal

Split black eye beans.

Gungo Peas

Known as pigeon peas or toovar.

Kala Chana

A ratter misshapen pale brown pea very similar to whole yellow peas in flavour.

Masoor Dhal

The skinned, salmon coloured split pea also known as red split lentils.

Moong Beans

A small, round, green bean, when sprouted produces the familiar beansprouts. Moong beans are one of the quicker cooking pulses and they may be cooked without soaking.

Red Chori

Red chori is a small, oval shaped, red pea with a wonderful nutty flavour. They are very similar in flavour to aduki beans and the two may happily be interchanged in recipes. Brown chori are also available.

Red Kidney Beans

Red kidney beans cook to a lovely 'mealy' texture. Soaking the beans reduces their toxicity but it may be entirely eliminated by ensuring that they boil vigorously for 10 minutes before lowering the heat and allowing them to simmer until tender.

Split Yellow Beans

Yellow beans which have been split with their skin removed have a pleasant, slightly sweet flavour and disintegrate when cooked.

Soya Beans

A very hard bean which requires long soaking and several hours cooking. Soya beans have the highest protein content of all the pulses.

Toovar Dhal

Also known as toovar dhal this is a skinned, dark ochre-coloured split pea with an earthy flavour.

Urad

A small black-skinned lentil of the same family as moong beans but with a slightly more bitter flavour.

Urad Dhal

Split, skinned urad is a pale creamy-beige colour.

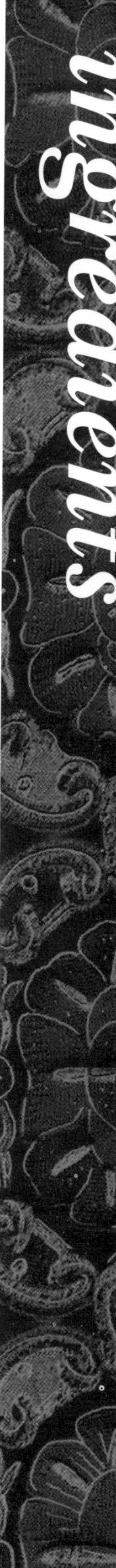

Vaal Beans

A small white bean, similar to haricot beans, with a slightly bitter flavour.

Vaal Dhal

Split vaal beans with the skin removed.

Dry Roasted Spices

This process heightens the aroma and flavour of whole spices such as coriander, cumin, fenugreek, mustard seeds, poppy seeds and sesame seeds. Gently heat a small, heavy frying pan (cast iron is ideal) and after 2 or 3 minutes put in the whole spices. Stir or shake the pan over a medium heat for several minutes until the spices change colour and give a lovely roasted fragrance.

Frying Spices

Indian cooking maximises the number of flavours from one spice by using it in many different ways. Whole, ground, dry-roasted or fried gently in oil or ghee. Many of the recipes in this book require you to fry whole or ground spices before adding other ingredients, a seemingly simple technique known as vaghar but one which requires care. Heat the oil over a medium heat, if it begins to smoke it is too hot. Some spices such as mustard seeds and sesame seeds splutter quite fiercely when they are ready so it is always better to cover the frying pan.

Ajmo

A native of southern India the seeds have little aroma until crushed when they become highly aromatic, reminiscent of thyme.

Anardana (Pomegranate Seeds)

The dried seeds of the pomegranate look rather like black raisins, have a slightly sour smell and distinctive sweet-sour taste. They are usually ground, or dry-roasted then ground and are use as a souring agent in chutneys, curries and braised vegetables as well as in filling for breads and savoury pastries.

Anise

Also known as aniseed this spice has a distinctive, liquorice-like smell and taste.

Asafoetida (Hing)

Asafoetida should be bought in small quantities since it is only ever used a pinch at a time and it must be stored in an airtight container to prevent its strong smell from dominating.

Cardammon (Elachi)

One of the most highly valued spices in the world after saffron. Like vanilla the pods are used as a flavouring and are not meant to be eaten, although chewing a few seeds sweetens and cleanses the breath. Cardammons are lightly aromatic and can enhance both sweet and savoury dishes. Ground cardammon is used so rarely it is better to grind your own.

Cassia Bark

A fairly coarse, flat red-brown bark which, being brittle, tends to break into short pieces. Its flavour is similar to cinnamon but far more intense which makes it better suited to India cooking.

Chillies

There are probably around 200 varieties of chilli grown in all parts of the tropics. If you want to reduce the fire try removing the seeds and veins. Pulverised fresh chillies freeze extremely well.

Chilli Powder

The chilli powder referred to in Asian cooking is ground red chillies. Its colour may vary from almost brick-red colour to vivid red depending on the type of chillies used.

Cloves

Look for cloves which are a reddish-brown colour on the stem and lighter on the crown. Good cloves will exude a small amount of oil if pressed with the fingernail. Ground cloves are one of the ingredients in garam masala.

Coriander (Dhania)

The fresh, green leaf of the coriander is popular for both flavouring and garnish in Middle Eastern as well as Asian cuisine and is well worth growing yourself

Cumin (Jeera)

Available both as whole seeds and in ground form the strong, heavy smell of cumin. In fact the combination of this with coriander leaves accounts for the characteristic smell of much Indian food. Cumin is one of the main constituents of curry powder as well as being essential in mixtures such as garam masala.

Curry Leaves (Karipulya)

Highly aromatic when fresh. Curry leaves are shaped a little like bay leaves.

Dhania Jeera

As its name suggests dhania jeera powder is a combination of roasted and ground coriander and cumin seeds used extensively in Gujarat style cooking. Whilst all dhania jeera mixes use more coriander than cumin the ratio may vary from four parts to one to two parts to one.

Fennel Seeds

Fennel seeds smell like aniseed and have a similar flavour although they are not as sweet. They are used principally in vegetarian cooking and may be dry-roasted and chewed after a meal as a mouth freshener and digestive.

Fenugreek (Methi)

The seeds are hard and flattish with a strong smell and bitter taste.

Garam Masala

A masala is a blend. It may contain just two or three spices and herbs or it could include a dozen or more. Garam masala is the principal spice blend of northern Indian cooking where every good cook will have their own favourite blend. Some blends, based on peppercorns and cloves are quite grey whilst others using cinnamon and cardammon are aromatic. All the recipes in this book use my sister Amina's special mix which she regularly sends for me. See page 14.

Ginger

Fresh ginger is now quite widely available. When buying it look for pieces with a taut fresh skin and store it in a cool airy place as you would garlic or onions. It must be peeled before being chopped or pulverised you will end up with a paste which may be frozen in an ice cube mould.

Garlic Paste

Garlic is one of the most widely used ingredients in the world. Used for countless preparations as well as its medical properties. Each clove of garlic is peeled and the flesh either chopped, grated or pulverised and made into paste.
When frying make sure the oil is not too hot or the garlic will burn and taste acrid. Garlic and ginger compliment each other and are often used together in recipes. Make the paste by pulverising the garlic and adding a spoon of salt and a little oil and lemon juice for preserving. Use as and when required.

Mustard Seeds (Rye)

Any Asian dish which includes mustard seeds is referring to the tiny reddish-brown seeds native to India. When popped into hot oil they have a delicious mild, nutty flavour.

Nutmeg

Buy whole nutmegs and grate them as required since the ground powder soon loses it flavour.

Poppy Seeds (Khus Khus)

Khus khus can become rancid so they should be kept in an airtight jar and stored in a cool place, you may even freeze them. Khus khus are sometimes ground and used as a thickening agent in Indian cooking.

Saffron (Kesar)

Saffron is the most expensive spice in the world. Always buy threads not ground saffron and look for a vibrant red-orange colour, deeper the colour the better the quality. Saffron has a highly aromatic flavour and a small quantity will flavour a large dish, turning it a brilliant gold.

Sesame Seeds (Tel)

Always buy the beige, unhulled seeds, not the common creamy-white ones. Sesame seeds have no essential oil and therefore no aroma but the flavour is mild, sweet and wonderfully nutty.

Tea Masala

A blend of mainly aromatic spices such as cardammon, cloves, cinnamon and ginger used in the classic Indian drink, spiced tea.
See page 14.

Turmeric

Generally only sold in its ground form, turmeric's colour indicates its quality. Its flavour is pungent, bitter and musky and it is an essential in curry powder.

Limbuphul

Citric acid is an organic acid found in many fruits.
It has no aroma but a pleasant and sour, acidic taste.
The grains of citric acid are sprinkled onto chewda's and snacks.
A good substitute for lemon juice adding a tang to the dish.

Agar-Agar

China grass is obtained from a variety of sea weed.
Sold as a thin crinkly, translucent white strips that have no aroma and hardly any taste. Can be bought in the powdered form too.

Jaggery

Ranges from mustard yellow to deep amber in colour, depending on the quality of the sugar cane juice.
It has a heavy caramel like aroma and a very sweet and musky taste.

Sago

Sago pearls are like small and hard white balls.
A close relative to tapioca and used for sweet and savoury dishes.
When cooked has the texture of caviar.

Aloe Bokhara

These are dried damsons which can be substituted with prunes.
Often used in speciality dinners or for serving at weddings.

Masalas

Here are a few selected recipes for fast cooking. They really come in handy when you want to cook from tinned foods such as fish or vegetables.

They can be used literally as one pleases. Each one stores well for almost a month in the fridge in glass bottles and can be used as required to your individual taste.

Sweet & Sour Paste

Ingredients

1 medium onion coarsely chopped
2 cloves garlic coarsely chopped
15ml - 1tbsp turmeric
30ml - 2tbsp coriander seeds
5ml - 1tsp ground chilli or to taste
5ml - ½tsp mustard seeds
5ml - 1tsp ground ginger
5ml - 1tsp cumin seeds
1.25ml - ¼tsp fenugreek seeds
vinegar to preserve the paste

Method

Put the onion and garlic in a blender, grind the spices together and combine. Add enough vinegar to make a stiff paste. Use as required.

Hot Paste

Ingredients

6 green chillies
½ inch fresh ginger
2 cloves garlic chopped
7.5ml - 1½tsp coriander seeds
5ml - 1tsp cumin seeds
1.25ml - ¼tsp turmeric
1.25ml - ¼tsp garam masala

Method

Grind all the ingredients together adding a little water to make a smooth paste.

Indian Curry Paste

Ingredients

4 dried red chillies
15ml - 4tbsp coriander seeds
15ml - 1tbsp cumin
15ml - 1tbsp mustard seeds
30ml - 2tbsp ground black pepper
30ml - 2tbsp coarse salt
7.5ml - ½tbsp saffron soaked in 45ml - 3tbsp boiling water
1 clove garlic crushed
4 fl oz - 125ml vinegar
2 fl oz - 65ml ghee

Method

Blend all the dry ingredients together. Combine in a blender with remaining ingredients and mix to a smooth paste.

Tandoori Masala

Ingredients

30ml - 6tsp cumin seeds
30ml - 6tsp coriander seeds
30ml - 6cm cinammon stick
15ml - 3tsp cloves
15ml - 3tsp chilli powder
15ml - 3tsp ginger powder
15ml - 3tsp turmeric
15ml - 3tsp garlic powder
15ml - 3tsp mace powder
15ml - 3tsp salt
5ml - 1tsp red food colouring

Method

Dry roast all the spices until they smoke, cool and grind with the powdered spices, salt and food colouring.
Can be used in masala or marinades. Mix with mayonnaise for an unusual dip.
Mix with yoghurt to marinate meat and poultry or even fish.
A little added to curries can do wonders for the appearance.

Garam Masala

Dry roasted aromatic whole spices, powdered and added to a dish for aromatic flavour, a pep up spice.

Ingredients

140g - 5oz coriander seeds
115g - 4oz cumin seeds
55g - 2oz black pepper corns
25g - 1oz cinammon
25g - 1oz black cardammons
15g - ½oz dry ginger powder
15g - ½oz mace
15g - ½oz bay leaves
(about 20)

Method

Mix together all the ingredients except the ginger powder.
Heat a wok or a heavy non stick fry pan. Add the mixed spices and stir continuously for a couple of minutes.
Remove from the heat and when cool grind to a fine powder. Add the ginger powder and mix well. Store in a airtight container in a dark place.

Easy Garam Masala

Ingredients

55g - 2oz black cardammon pods
140g - 5oz cumin seeds
25g - 1oz cinammon sticks
25g - 1oz cloves
25g - 1oz black pepper corns
4 bayleaves

Method

Crush open the black cardammon pod and extract the tiny seeds inside.
Put the cardammon seeds, cumin seeds, cinammon sticks, cloves, peppercorns and bayleaves in a processor until a fine powder forms.

Instant Tea Masala

Ingredients

55g - 2oz ginger powder
55g - 2oz cinammon powder
25g - 1oz ground cardammon
2tsp - 10ml white pepper
4tsp - 20ml black pepper

Method

Mix all the ingredients well together and store in an airtight tin.
Use as required.

A selection of spices used in the recipes

A variety of savouries

Meat Samosa

Think of Indian food and immediately the samosa springs to mind. No other food is more commonly seen in shops and restaurants.
With a little practice even the inexperienced cook will be able to turn out perfect triangles.
Admittedly making samosa is time consuming but a demonstration of the process proves that they are not as time consuming as they say.
With each attempt you will get better and perfect triangular shapes will be the result. For convenience and ease a ready made pastry known as pur can be bought, this cuts time in half. Be sure that corners are not left gaping as even the tiniest hole will allow oil to seep through when frying resulting in soggy and unattractive samosa.

Ingredients (for the filling)

30ml - 2tbsp cooking oil
900g - 2lb chicken or lamb mince, washed and drained
2 large onions, chopped fine
8-10 green chillies, washed and pounded fine
15ml - 3tsp ginger paste
10ml - 2tsp garlic paste
12.5ml - 2½tsp salt
30ml - 6tsp coriander powder
2.5ml - ½tsp turmeric
2.5ml - ½tsp garam masala
1 bunch fresh green coriander
1 bunch green shallots or spring onions, washed and chopped fine

Method

Braise mince in pan with oil. Add salt and turmeric. When moisture has evaporated add ginger, green chillies and coriander powder.
Stir frequently to avoid lumps. When cooked add onions and braise just enough until moisture has evaporated.
Allow to cool. Add chopped greens and garam masala.

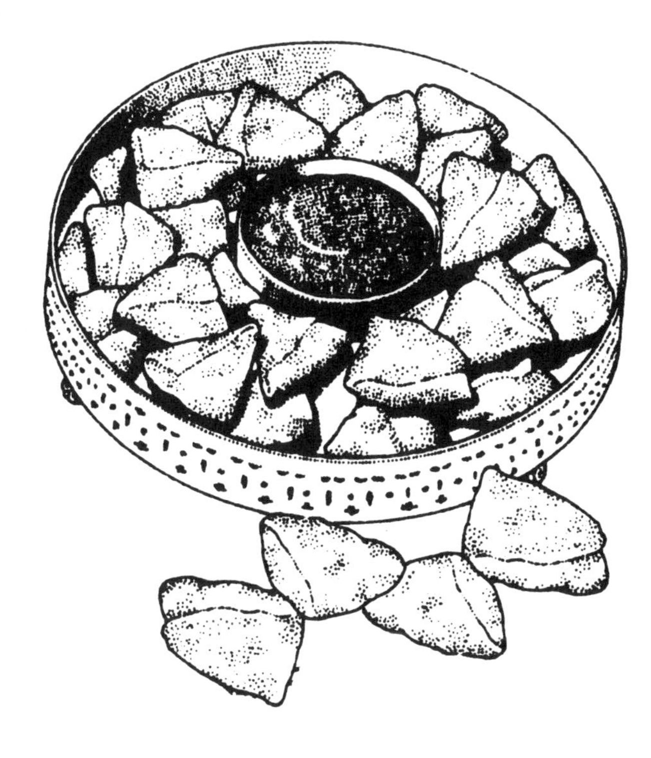

Ingredients for 'pur' (pastry)

1 kg - 2lb 4oz plain flour
A good pinch of salt
30ml - 2tbsp lemon juice

Method

Boil water and make a fairly stiff dough with the above ingredients. The lemon juice gives a crispy pastry known as 'pur'.
Make small balls from the dough. Roll into 6-8cm discs. Put 4 discs in a stack, brushing each well on both sides with vegetable oil and sprinkling flour in between. Only the underside of the bottom disc and the top side of the top disc must not be greased.
Now roll the stack out into a large circle, turning over and rolling both the top and bottom side a few times.
Put the stacks on a hot griddle, turning and being careful not to brown. The layers begin to separate as the heat enters. Neatly pile the discs on top of each other and start the next stack.
Experienced cooks can handle up to 8 discs at a time.
When cool trim the sides and cut pastry into strips.
Place the prepared filling on each strip and fold into triangles. The edge should be sealed with a little of the paste made from 90ml - 6 tbsp of flour and 90ml - 6 tbsp of water.
The samosas are now ready to freeze or fry. About six dozens can be made from this recipe. Serve with lemon and chutney.

Vegetable Samosa

Samosas are particularly apt for the Muslim holy month of Ramadan.
These savoury triangles are filled with either minced meat or vegetables, deep-fried and served as a starter.
Beginners are often put off making samosas because they assume it is a laborious and complicated process.
However, although samosas can be time consuming, once you get into the practice of making them, you will have perfect triangles.
All the effort will have been worthwhile as the results are the tastiest of savouries.

Ingredients

900g - 2lb packet of frozen mixed vegetables
2 medium onions
2 medium potatoes
1 small round cabbage
½ bunch spring onions
½ bunch fresh coriander
10/12 fresh green chillies
30ml - 2tbsp fresh garlic
30ml - 2tbsp mustard seeds
45ml - 3tbsp cooking oil
2.5ml - ½tsp citric acid
6 karipulya leaves
salt to taste
15ml - 1tbsp coriander powder
2.5ml - ½tsp garam masala

Method

Pour the oil in a large pan and switch on the heat. Add the mustard seeds and karipulya leaves and cover until they stop spluttering. Add garlic paste and green chillies which have been pounded together until fine and stir for a few minutes. Add the vegetables, the potato which has been peeled and the remaining spices. Stir well and cook on medium heat. Meanwhile in a processor finely shred the cabbage and onions and when the potatoes are almost cooked add the cabbage and onions. Cook until all the moisture has evaporated. Switch off and cool completely. Gently stir in the chopped greens and garam masala.
By this time the pastry should have defrosted. Separate the layers and fill each strip with the mixture, folding the triangle over until you reach the end of the strip. Stick the end down with the paste made from 30ml - 6tsp of plain flour and 30ml - 6tsp of water.
Fry in deep oil until golden. Serve with fresh lemon wedges and chutney.

Vegetable & Nut Samosa

Ingredients

350g - 12oz potatoes peeled and diced
100g - 4oz frozen peas
45ml - 3tbsp vegetable oil
1 small onion chopped
5ml - 1tsp ginger paste
5ml - 1tsp garlic paste
5ml - 1tsp garam masala
2.5ml - ½tsp cumin seeds
2tsp lemon juice
2.5ml -½tsp mustard seeds
55g - 2oz unsalted cashew nuts coarsely chopped
vegetable oil for shallow frying
salt
coriander leaves

Pastry

280g - 10oz plain flour
55g - 2oz margarine
75ml - 5tbsp warm milk

Method

Cook the potatoes in a pan of boiling salted water. Add the potato and peas mixture and cook from a few minutes longer.
Drain well. In a pan heat the oil and fry the onion and add all the spices and the potatoes and peas. Stir in the lemon juice and cook gently, remove from the heat and slightly crush the peas and potatoes, add the cashew nuts and season with salt.

For the pastry rub the marg into the flour and make a firm dough with the milk.
Divide into 6 balls and roll a 7" circle, cutting each in half.
Divide the filling equally and brush the edges with water and seal well.
Fry in hot oil and drain well.
Serve with chutneys and lemon slices.

Potato Bhajia

Ingredients

1 small potato - cut into tiny cubes
1 small onion sliced thinly
6 green chillies
4 cloves garlic and 15ml - 1tbsp yoghurt all processed together
115g - 4oz fresh spinach chopped fine
2.5ml - ½tsp mustard seeds
30ml - 2tbsp fresh coriander chopped fine
5ml - 1tsp salt
2.5ml - ½tsp turmeric
5ml - 1tsp coriander powder
2.5ml - ½tsp cumin powder
15ml - 1tbsp vegetable oil
15ml - 1tbsp rice flour
5ml - 1tsp baking powder
2.5ml - ½tsp asafoetida
175g - 6oz gram flour
add cold water to make a medium consistency batter
oil for frying

Method

Mix all the ingredients together, add enough water gradually to make a batter. Heat oil on a medium heat, fry spoonfuls of batter to make the bhajia, they should rise and become round.
Fry turning occasionally and remove with a slotted spoon.
Serve with chutneys.

Garlic & Mushroom Bhajia

Ingredients

1½ cups gram flour
2.5ml - ½tsp salt
2.5ml - ½tsp baking powder
5ml - 1tsp cumin powder
5ml - 1tsp chilli powder
½ cup cold water
2 cloves garlic peeled and crushed
1 small onion peeled and finely chopped
vegetable oil for frying
450g - 1lb button mushrooms trimmed and cleaned

Method

Mix together the flour, salt, baking powder, cumin and chilli powder. Make a well in the centre of the mixture and gradually stir in enough water, mixing to form a medium consistency batter.
Stir in the garlic and onion and leave for 15 minutes.
Heat the oil until, fairly hot then mix in the mushrooms a few at a time coating well with the batter and fry in small batches. Drain with a slotted spoon and serve with a green chutney.

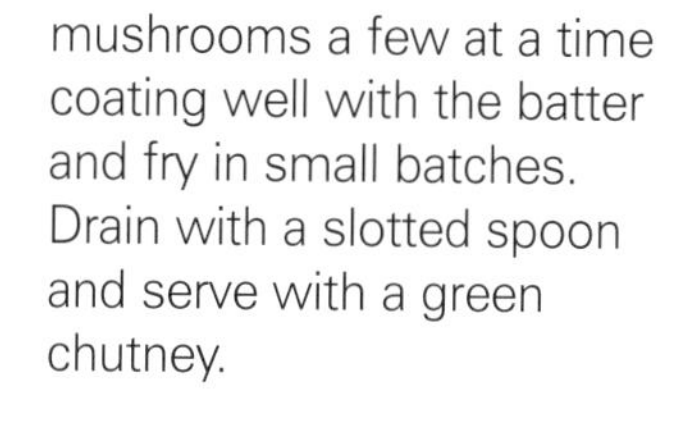

Dodhi Lagan

The thousand or so species of cucurbitaceae (the marrow family) are mainly rapidly growing climbing plants from the warmer and tropical countries of the world. They are rich in vitamins A and C as well as trace elements. Marrows belong to one of the oldest plant families on earth. The more common family members are cucumber, pumpkin, wax gourd and the custard marrow. Zucchinis are immature vegetable marrows. All marrows are at their best when small and their flesh is delicate and tender. In Asian cuisine the marrow is often called the dodhi. Like the potato, it is a versatile vegetable. It can be used in spicy and savoury dishes as well as in sweet puddings. Combining with meat or other vegetables, you can transform the humble marrow into a gastronomic delight.
The colour of this vegetable ranges from dark green to a paler shade. Even creamy yellow varieties are grown. However, the flesh is not influenced by the colour of the skin. Try this recipe for dodhi lagan over which poppy seeds are scattered to give the dish a lovely golden and attractive finish. Sliced into diamond shapes, served hot or cold, you will soon add it to your list of favourites.

Ingredients

60ml - 4tbsp vegetable oil
1 beaten egg
75ml - 2.5 fl oz milk
25g - 1oz gram flour
25g - 1oz corn flour
55g - 2oz self-raising flour
10ml - 2tsp baking powder
125ml - 4 fl oz milk
1 grated onion
175g - 6oz peeled and grated dodhi (marrow)
45ml - 3tbsp chopped fresh coriander
salt to taste
few pounded green chillies (more for extra hotness)
2.5ml - ½tsp cumin powder
2.5ml - ½tsp garlic paste
poppy seeds or sesame seeds (for topping and decoration)

Method

Mix together all the above ingredients except the baking powder, flour and poppy or sesame seeds. When the mixture is blended together well, add the flours, which have been sifted together with the baking powder. Fold in gently. Grease an oven dish or casserole at least 5cm - 2 inches deep. Gently pour in the mixture. Bake at gas mark 5 (180°C/350F) in a pre-heated oven for almost half an hour or until light golden. Brush with the beaten egg and liberally sprinkle with poppy seeds or sesame seeds over the top of the lagan for decoration. Continue to bake for another 10 minutes. Remove from the oven and slice. Serve hot or cold with chutneys and relishes.

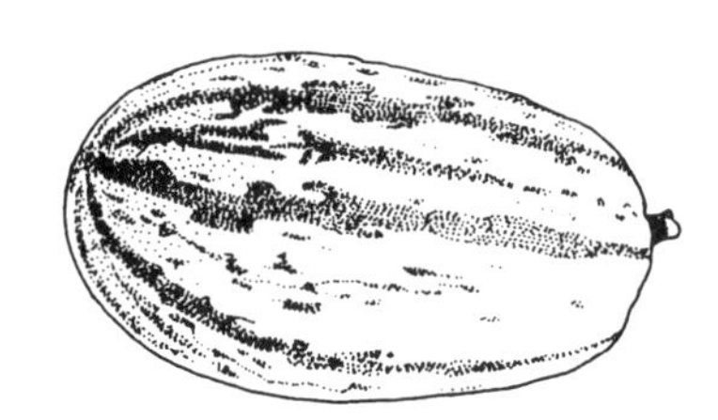

Fish Sticks

Fish - so rich in vitamins, oil and proteins has an important role to play in any diet. it can be cooked in many ways, baked, fried, curried or even barbecued. The options are almost endless.
Fish mongers nowadays are extremely helpful. They are willing to clean and prepare the fish you buy to your individual requirements. If you take advantage of this service, today's recipe, fish sticks, can be prepared in next to no time. Fish sticks are best eaten hot. They are quickly fried and full of nutrition. Mint chutney provides the ideal dip.

Ingredients

225g - 8oz white fish steaks cubed coley or cod
½ bunch fresh coriander
8 green chillies pureed with a little lime juice
60ml - 4tbsp plain flour
15ml - 1tbsp chick pea flour
2.5ml - ½tsp salt
2.5ml - ½tsp turmeric
10ml - 2tsp fresh garlic paste
2.5ml - ½tsp mint sauce
2 beaten eggs and breadcrumbs for coating

Method

Mix all ingredients. Marinate the fish in the mix for a few hours or even overnight. Pierce the cubes with cocktails sticks, dip in the beaten eggs, to which salt and pepper has been added, and coat with bread crumbs. Fry in deep hot oil delicious eaten hot with mint chutney!

Chicken & Corn Lagan

The Indian thali is used to serve a meal or for baking in the oven. Today, any oven-cooked meal is termed lagan. As with most savouries and desserts prepared for lunches, dinners or formal occasions, a wide variety of lagans can be served, be it sweet or savoury, with meat or vegetarian. The various methods of cooking are not all that different and yet they have their own distinctive taste according to the ingredients used. Cut into diamond shapes a lagan provides an attractive slice as well as being delicious, whether eaten hot or cold and served with chutney or ambli (tamarind) sauce.

Ingredients

1 small tin cream-style sweetcorn
55g - 2oz butter
55g - 2oz chicken pieces cut very small and washed
3 eggs
salt to taste
3 green chillies & 3 cloves garlic pounded into a paste
1.25ml - ¼tsp white pepper
1.25ml - ¼tsp coriander powder
30ml - 2tbsp self-raising flour
15ml - 1tbsp oil
½ pinch fresh coriander
1 beaten egg white
khus khus (poppy seeds)

Method

Brown the chicken in a little oil with salt.
Into a blender, crack the eggs and add the butter, chillies and garlic, fresh coriander and salt.
Blend for a few minutes until frothy. Pour out into a mixing bowl, add the rest of the spices, mix in the chicken and sweetcorn and finally fold in the flour that has been sifted.
Pour into a greased baking sheet and bake at gas mark 5 (180°C) for 30 minutes or until set and golden brown.
In the last five minutes before removing from the oven, brush with beaten egg white and sprinkle poppy seeds over the top for decoration.

Creamed Chicken Sticks

Ramadan is a blessed month for Muslims who fast from sunrise to sunset. Special savoury foods are prepared in advance and frozen so that, when the holy month arrives, as much time as possible can be devoted to prayer.
It is a good idea to keep savouries in the freezer throughout the year because they make excellent starters when friends or family drop in unexpectedly for a cup of tea. They are thoroughly appreciated on cold winter evenings.

Ingredients

2 chicken breasts, washed and sliced lengthways into strips
2 eggs, whisked
breadcrumbs for coating

Marinade

blend together one tin of Nestle sterilised cream
½ bunch fresh green coriander
4 green chillies
2 dried red chillies
10ml - 2tsp salt
10ml - 2tsp yoghurt
15ml - 3tsp coriander powder
10ml - 2tsp fresh garlic paste
5ml - 1tsp ginger paste
oil for frying

Method

Blend ingredients for marinade until very smooth. Coat the chicken strips with the paste and marinate overnight in a covered container. In the morning, pierce the chicken strips right through with cocktail sticks. Then dip in the beaten egg to which a little salt has been added. Dip the chicken in breadcrumbs and place on a tray. Shallow fry in vegetable oil. Serve hot with lemon slices and chutney.
This appetiser can also be frozen successfully by open freezing on a tray. Place in a container when hard.
There is no need to thaw the pieces before cooking. They can be fried on medium heat straight from the freezer.

Khandvi

Impress your friends with this starter and they will come back for more.
Well worth the hard work and the taste is delicious.

Ingredients

85g - 3oz gram flour
5ml - 1tsp salt
5ml - 1tsp grated ginger
2.5ml - ½tsp turmeric
2.5ml - ½tsp chilli powder
175ml - 6 fl oz yoghurt
450ml - 16 fl oz water

Garnish

45ml - 3tbsp oil
15ml - 1tbsp black mustard seeds
15ml - 1tbsp sesame seeds
45ml - 3tbsp fresh coriander chopped
30ml - 2tbsp desiccated coconut
red chilli for sprinkling

Method

Mix together the gram flour salt chilli and turmeric in a large bowl.
Whisk the yoghurt and water together and then gradually incorporate the liquid into the dry ingredients. In a non stick sauce pan cook the mixture over a medium heat for about 30 minutes. Stir continuously test to see if it is cooked by spreading a little of the paste onto the plate and after a few seconds you should be able to lift and roll the mixture. Spread the paste thinly over a greased working surface or a thali, with a spatula and cut into 2" strips and roll into small Swiss roll shapes. Arrange on a platter. Heat oil in a small pan and add the mustard and sesame seeds, when spluttering has stopped pour the hot oil over the khandvi and garnish with remaining ingredients.

Dhokra

What would Indian cuisine be without savouries? With an endless variety to choose from dhokra play a leading role and are always popular. Using ingredients that are commonly available, dhokra are ideal for serving guests or visiting friends.
Dhokra are made with gram flour, a very pale flour and from one of the varieties of chick peas, usually the kale chana. The final topping of seeds and coconut add that special touch as well as the crunch. Dhokra are best described as squares of steamy savoury cake. They are usually eaten warm with a green chutney. These are a gujarati speciality and a must at buffets and other occasions.

Ingredients

225g - 8oz gram flour
25g - 1oz fine semolina
2 green chillies chopped
2.5ml - ½tsp turmeric
5ml - 1tsp salt
5ml - 1tsp sugar
5ml - 1tsp ginger paste
175ml - 6 fl oz water
175ml - 6 fl oz yoghurt
15ml - 1tbsp oil
2.5ml - ½tsp bicarb of soda
2.5ml - ½tsp Eno fruit salts

For decoration

6ml - 4tbsp oil
5ml - 1tsp cumin seeds
10ml - 2tsp mustard seeds
10ml - 2tsp sesame seeds
10ml - 2tsp desiccated coconut
30ml - 2tbsp freshly chopped coriander
5ml - 1tsp chilli powder

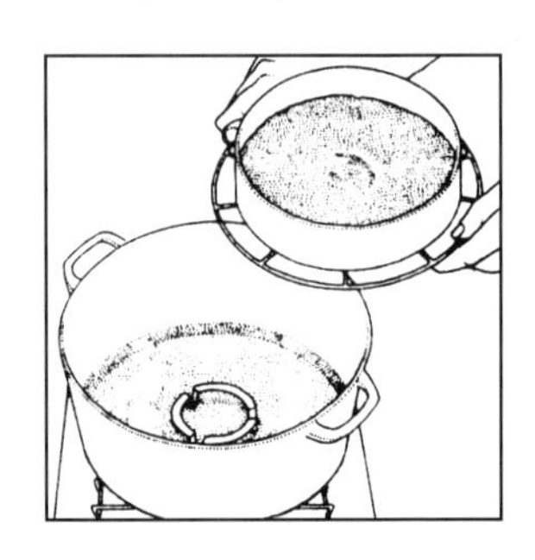

Method

Sift the flour into a bowl, add the semolina, salt, turmeric, sugar, green chilli and ginger. Mix thoroughly. Whisk together the yoghurt and the water and stir in the other ingredients, leaving aside the oil and bicarb of soda. Cover with a damp cloth and leave for a few hours. Divide the batter into half. Mixing half of the Eno into one half pour into a greased 8" sandwich tin and steam for 12 minutes on a medium heat, allow to cool in the tin.
Mix the remaining Eno into the other half and carry out the same procedure.
Heat oil in a saucepan and add all the topping ingredients, stir for a few minutes and allow the seeds to pop. Pour onto the squares and sprinkle the fresh coriander and chilli powder.

Relish Fritters

Ingredients

55g - 2oz plain flour
2.5ml - ½tsp coriander powder
2.5ml - ½tsp cumin seeds
1.25ml - ¼tsp chilli powder
2.5ml - ½tsp turmeric
1.25ml - ¼tsp salt
1 egg
45ml - 3tbsp milk
350g - 12oz potatoes
2 garlic cloves crushed
5 spring onions trimmed and chopped
55g - 2oz sweetcorn kernels
vegetable oil

Relish

1 onion
250g - 9oz tinned tomatoes
30ml - 2tbsp chopped fresh mint
30ml - 2tbsp chopped fresh coriander
30ml - 2tbsp lemon juice
2.5ml - ½tsp roasted cumin seeds
1.25ml - ¼tsp salt
1.25ml - ¼tsp paprika

Method

Make the relish by cutting the onion and tomatoes into small cubes and mixing in the remaining ingredients. Leave aside for 15 minutes to allow the flavours to incorporate with each other.
In a bowl sieve the flour and stir in the spices and salt and make a well in the centre add the whisked egg and milk and mix to make a batter.
Coarsely grate the potatoes and run under the tap in a sieve to get rid of excess starch. Drain and squeeze the moisture out. Stir into the batter with spring onions garlic and corn. Heat about a tablespoon of oil in a frying pan and add a few tablespoons of mixture at a time. They should be slightly flattened fry turning occasionally to make a crispy batter. Remove with a slotted spoon and drain well.
Serve hot with your choice of chutney.

Wara

A delicious spicy pancake flavoured with fresh coriander very easy to make and delicious eaten hot.

Ingredients

450g - 1lb gram flour
10ml - 2tsp ajwain
5ml - 1tsp chilli powder
1.25ml - ¼tsp black pepper
1.25ml - ¼tsp asafoetida
1 tomato skinned and finely chopped
1 small grated onion
700ml - 1¼pt water
7.5ml - 1¼tsp salt
30ml - 2tbsp fresh coriander

Method

Sift the flour and mix together all the remaining ingredients to form a smooth batter. Leave aside for 30 minutes.
In a non stick pan lightly oiled drop spoonfuls to make small circles and cook for 40 to 50 seconds on each side until golden brown.
Alternately make large circles like pancakes filling the pan up, turn carefully.
When golden, cool on a wire rack.

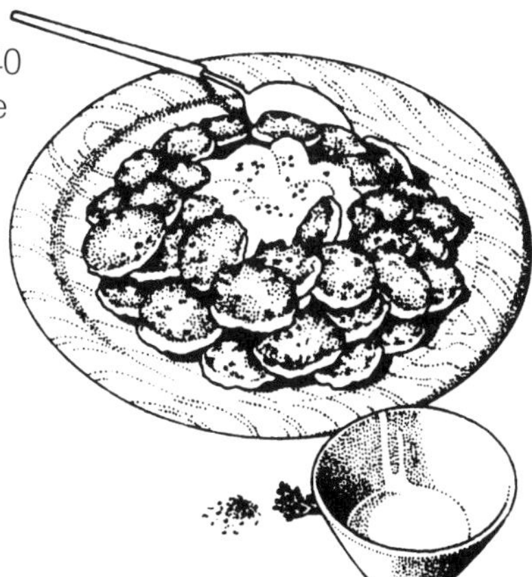

Potato & Chicken Plaits

Young or old, everyone is fond of savouries, these dishes play a central part in Asian cuisine and informal entertaining. Savouries serve as the gateway to a main meal. There are many varieties. Add the ease of using ready made pastry saving a great deal of time and effort. The fillings are variable. Those who do not eat meat can substitute extra vegetables instead or even use soya meat or quorn. The shapes of the pastries are up to the individual. It is fun to experiment and be creative. Be adventurous by using assorted decorations, poppy seeds, onion seeds and even sesame seeds. Look around the supermarkets shelves and experiment with the endless varieties available.
Folding a plait can be tricky if you are a beginner but don't give up. With time and practice, it will be like child's play.

Ingredients

450g - 1lb chicken breasts, cubed
2 medium sized onions, finely grated
2 medium potatoes, cubed
8 green chillies
15ml - 3tsp garlic paste
2.5ml - ½tsp cumin seeds
55g - 2oz margarine
salt and pepper to taste
115g - 4oz grated cheese
1 packet frozen puff pastry
85g - 3oz fresh green coriander, chopped
1 egg yolk, beaten well
sesame seeds for decoration

Method

Melt the margarine in a pan. Add the chicken, potatoes and cumin seeds. Stir for a while then add the spices and salt. Stir well, lower the heat and cover. Stir occasionally until cooked when cooked mix in the cheese and fresh coriander. Mix well.
Meanwhile the pastry should have defrosted. Roll out into two oblong shapes, cut the sides straight to make them neat. Slit from the sides (like an upside down V) but be sure not to cut through completely. Line the filling down the centre and start folding in the pastry like a plait. Glaze with the egg yolk and sprinkle with the sesame seeds. Bake in a hot oven. Slice when warm and serve with a green chutney.

Batata Pawa

Pawa look like rice that have been flattened, but they are actually made by a similar process to that as making corn flakes.
They are truly delicious combined with potato and spices to make the traditional gujarati favourite snack of batata pawa.
This dish can be served hot as a starter or as a light dish with green chutney or yoghurt.
The super thing about is it that this recipe takes so little time to prepare.

Ingredients

175g - 6oz pawa
2 medium potatoes, cubed
2.5ml - ½tsp cumin seeds
5ml - 1tsp sesame seeds
5ml - 1tsp mustard seeds
5ml - 1tsp salt
2.5ml - ½tsp turmeric
2.5ml - ½tsp chilli powder
2.5ml - ½tsp garam masala
¼ cup hot water
60ml - 4tbsp oil
55g - 2oz butter
30ml - 2tbsp lemon juice
5ml - 1tsp sugar
karipulya leaves
lots of fresh green coriander for the garnish

Method

Boil the potatoes until they are just cooked. Meanwhile wash the pawa in cold water and leave to drain.
Heat the oil in a large pan and add cumin, sesame seeds and mustard seeds.
When the seeds have stopped spluttering, add the leaves and potatoes. Stir frequently for 3 minutes. Add the remaining spices and cook for a minute longer.
Sprinkle lemon juice, sugar and pawa into the frying pan, mix well and add the hot water and butter, then cook for another few minutes until the mixture has been thoroughly mixed and is piping hot.
Serve in a dish garnished with chopped coriander leaves.

Chicken & Cheese Delights

Ingredients

2 chicken breasts, washed and cut into cube-size pieces
2 medium sized onions, finely sliced
3 small potatoes cut into small cubes
6 green chillies
15ml - 3tsp garlic paste
10ml - 2tsp coriander powder
5ml - 1tsp mustard seeds
2.5ml - ½tsp turmeric
55g - 2oz butter
salt to taste
115g - 4oz vegetarian Irish cheddar cheese
1 packet fresh or frozen puff pastry
fresh green coriander
1 egg, separated
sesame seeds for sprinkling

Method

Melt the butter in a frying pan and add the mustard seeds. When the seeds have stopped popping, add onions and garlic. Cook on low heat, stirring occasionally. Do not let the onion go brown. Add the chicken, potatoes and other spices. Mix thoroughly and cook on low heat, stirring now and again until the chicken and potatoes are cooked. This stage can also be done in a 650-watt microwave oven. Cook for 10 minutes on full power but remember to stir frequently. When the mixture is cooked, and while still hot, stir in the grated cheese and add finely chopped green coriander. Stir and cool.
Roll out the pastry and fill with the mixture, sealing the edges well with the egg white. The yolk can be used for the glaze before baking. A variety of shapes can be made- triangles or a roll which can be cut into bite-size pieces or even a boat shape by cutting a square, filling the middle and folding one corner in and overlapping the opposite corner, leaving the other two corners open. Bake for 20 minutes in a hot oven.
These savouries are easy to freeze. When frozen hard put them in a container. Bake from frozen with beaten egg yolk for the glaze and sprinkle with sesame seeds. If you have some mixture left over bake some vol-au-vent cases in a hot oven for 10 minutes. Add the filling when cool.

Frozen, uncooked vol-au-vent cases are available from supermarkets. They are an absolute boon to the busy cook. It is easy to take them from the packet and pop them in a hot oven. The results are perfectly shaped and beautifully risen vol-au-vents every time.

Stuffed Chicken Bites

Ingredients

3 chicken breasts
115g - 4oz chicken mince
15ml - 1tbsp oil
5ml - 1tsp garlic paste
5ml - 1tsp ginger paste
15ml - 1tbsp plain flour
15ml - 1tbsp butter
30ml - 2tbsp tomato puree
2.5ml - ½tsp cardammon powder
2.5ml - ½tsp garam masala
¼ cup grated pineapple
½ bunch parsley chopped fine
60ml - 2tbsp finely chopped green chillies
15ml - 1tbsp ground cashew nuts
5ml - 1tsp salt

Method

Heat the oil in a pan and add the ginger/garlic paste. Sauté on low heat till golden brown add the flour and fl of the tomato puree, green chilli and keep stirring until the mixture has thickened. Keep the sauce aside. Grate the pineapple and dry roast in a pan for 2 minutes to remove excess moisture, remove from the heat and add the remaining tomato puree. Also add the garam masala powder, butter chopped parsley, chicken mince cashew nuts, garlic and salt to taste. Mix well and keep the filling aside.

Pat dry the washed chicken breasts. Slit them and stuff with the filling, deep each in the sauce till well coated, wrap in baking foil and bake in a hot oven for 12 minutes or till well cooked and tender. Serve hot with a chutney of your choice.

Savoury Crescents

With the amazing variety of gadgets available nowadays, cooking seems so much fun and more interesting.
I came across this plastic gadget for making crescent or triangular shapes in pastry, which one can fill with either sweet or savoury fillings.
Bake or fry them - the savouries retain a lovely clear-cut shape and, amazingly, they are faster to make than the traditional methods.
In this recipe I have used the crescent-shaped gadgets to make these savouries which can be filled with a mixture of your choice.
Whether vegetarian or non-vegetarian, you can be sure it will be a delicious, perfectly shaped starter, or just simply something to serve with tea that will never fail to satisfy.
It may sound like a laborious and time-consuming process, but it really isn't that complicate.
There are simpler methods of making the pastry, which admittedly can be used.
However, occasionally one should be adventurous and experiment with different techniques.
Trust in yourself and gain that confidence, for cooking and entertaining is an art in itself-and remember: practice makes perfect!

Ingredients

225g - 8oz minced meat, chicken or lamb, or vegetarian soya meat
2.5ml - ½tsp ginger paste
2.5ml - ½tsp garlic paste
5ml - 1tsp green chillies (ground)
2.5ml - ½tsp coriander powder
1.25ml - ¼tsp turmeric
5ml - 1tsp salt
1 medium onion (finely chopped)
30ml - 2tbsp chopped coriander
225g - 8oz mixed vegetables (frozen)

15ml - 1tbsp butter
a good pinch each of turmeric, red chilli powder, cumin/coriander powder
salt & pepper

30ml - 2tbsp plain flour
60ml - 4tbsp water
5ml - 1tsp vinegar

Method

Cook meat with first set of spices and onion until moisture evaporates. Stir often breaking up any lumps.
Fold in fresh coriander and steam vegetables in very little water until tender.
Drain.
Melt the butter, add second set of spices. Boil together flour, water and vinegar on gentle heat, take care to avoid lumps.
Once boiled, pour over the vegetables and combine with the meat mixture.

Pastry Ingredients

30ml - 2tbsp butter
225ml - 8 fl oz water
115g - 4oz plain flour
breadcrumbs
3 eggs
oil for deep-frying

Method

Melt butter and water and bring to the boil. Remove from heat and add flour at once.
Lower heat and return to cooker.
Cook, stirring vigorously until mixture leaves sides and forms a ball. Cool.
Divide into three. Roll out thinly and fill crescent-shaped gadget with filling.
Close together and press edges to seal.
Dip onto beaten egg, roll in breadcrumbs and fry in deep hot oil.

There is almost no end to the varieties on offer as far as Indian food is concerned. Savouries can be made from the large variety of lentils available, flours ground from dhal (lentils) and beans and from meat and vegetables. Some cultural occasions call for certain snacks, such as pakoras or chevda at tea parties and chana batata or even bher puri when something more filling is required.
Savouries are also eaten during Indian wedding festivities, which can stretch over a week.
The delicious items also provide a welcome break at mehendi (henna) parties.
Traditionally, samosas are used as starters or snacks. This hors d'oeuvre has been popular for many generations.
Patras are madumbi (yam) leaves that have had their veins removed, spread with batter, rolled, steamed and fried.
Patras are very similar to the dolmas of the Greeks and Turks who stuff grape leaves using slightly different ingredients but the same method.

Ingredients

24 madumbi leaves
350g - 12oz gram flour
115g - 4oz rice flour
75ml - 5tbsp yoghurt
3 medium sized onions, finely chopped or grated
60ml - 4tbsp ambli- tamarind mixed with water
15ml - 1tbsp achar masala (pickle paste)
60ml - 4tbsp ground green chillies
¼ bunch chopped fresh coriander
30ml - 2tbsp crushed garlic
10ml - 2tsp margarine
15ml - 1tbsp turmeric
30ml - 2tbsp coriander powder
5ml - 1tsp garam masala
30ml - 2tbsp sesame seeds
15ml - 1tbsp desiccated coconut
30ml - 2tbsp salt

Method

Remove the veins from the leaves, wash and drain. Mix all the ingredients to make a paste, not too thick or thin but easy to spread on the leaves.
The liquid should be sufficient to make the batter but, if more is required, add hot water to the tamarind and squeeze out more juice.
Place the leaves in piles of six.
Spread the mixture on each leaf before covering with another. Apply the batter on the side with the veins, fold in the two long sides about 3.5cm - 1.5 inches from the edge. Spread more batter and then fold in the two rounded edges. Apply batter evenly over the edges and roll all the leaves tightly (like a swiss roll) from that end towards the pointed end.
For larger leaves divide in piles of four with the larger ones at the bottom.
Spread the batter evenly. Do not fold in the sides but pile the next one on and continue so forth until all four are spread with batter.
Then fold in the sides and rounded edges, all four leaves together. Smear with batter and roll tightly towards the pointed end.
Steam for at least three quarters of an hour until the colour of the leaves changes to a lighter shade. Test with a knife to ensure the middle is cooked. Steamed patra, eaten without frying, are delicious as well as being low in calories.
However, sliced and fried, patra are even tastier. They are difficult to resist served with drinks or desserts, making ideal snacks for tea time.
Patra also freeze very well after being steamed and sliced.
To store them in this way place the slices in containers with foil in between the layers of slices to separate them. When required for use, defrost them in a microwave or at room temperature. They are then ready to fry.

Chickpeas & New Potatoes

With new potatoes available it is rather difficult to resist buying them. They are so tender and cook very quickly. The humble potato is used in numerous different recipes. In this recipe chickpeas and tamarind are added to potatoes to make a popular dish eaten in many households.
This dish is commonly served at dinner parties and at get-togethers. Each cook or host has an individual recipe.
Chickpeas have been produced for centuries in the Middle East. There are two well-known varieties white and black.
The white is hard and shaped like a hazelnut. It has a nuttier flavour and a crunchy texture. Eaten whole or ground into flour.
White chickpeas are also used to make the Middle Eastern dip known as hummous.
They double in size when soaked. Thoroughly boiled, they are often eaten in salads and stews.

Ambli (tamarind), the other vital ingredient for this dish, has a very sharp taste. It can transform the whole taste of a dish.
Rust brown and even blackish tamarind pods contain up to ten compartments, each with a seed embedded in a dry, even pith.
This pith comprises as much as 16% organic acids. Tamarind is grown in India, Indonesia and several African countries.
Its juice is extracted by removing the outer skin, soaking the pips and pith in water and pressing the mass through a sieve to obtain a thick liquid.
This recipe can be adjusted- by varying the amount of chillies - to obtain the degree of hotness desired.

Ingredients

900g - 2lb small new potatoes
450g - 1lb white chickpeas, cooked (or 3 cans chickpeas)
45ml - 3tbsp tomato puree
105ml - 7tbsp tomato sauce
45ml - 3tbsp cooking oil
15ml - 1tbsp mustard seed
30ml - 2tbsp salt
30ml - 2tbsp chilli powder
5ml - 1tsp turmeric
15ml - 1tbsp hot pepper sauce
30ml - 2tbsp tamarind pulp

Method

Peel, wash and cube the potatoes and place in pre-boiled water. Boil on medium heat.
While the potatoes are boiling, drain the chickpeas and, in a separate saucepan, heat the oil.
Throw in the mustard seeds and curry leaves. Cover with a lid and allow the ingredients to stop spluttering.
Then add the tomato puree, tomato sauce, salt, chillies, hot pepper sauce and turmeric.
Stir for a few minutes until a wonderful colour appears and then switch off.
Remove the potatoes from the heat when they are just cooked.
Wash and drain.
Place the pan on low heat again.
Add the potatoes and the chickpeas to the tomato mixture and stir carefully.
Then add the juice extracted from the pulp of the tamarind.
Allow to boil once again and then switch off. Taste for salt.
The dish is now ready to serve.

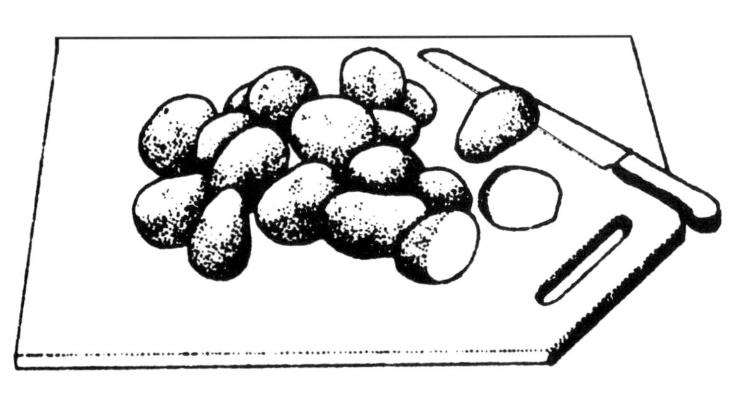

Sev

It is difficult to believe that anything so simple could taste so delicious. The ingredients for sev just takes a few minutes to prepare and a few moments more to fry. The gadget used to push these thin savouries out is an interesting gadget in itself.
Usually a brass colour with three or four different templates of assorted sizes, the machine is available from most Asian supermarkets.
The top has a handle which when turned, moves along in a spiral motion. This squeezes out the flour dough which is then dropped into the hot oil. The preparation time for this sev is minimal as the oil needed for frying can be put to heat while the flour is prepared. The dough is extremely light and is made from gram flour.

Sev has a crunchy savoury taste, and is often mixed with bhers or chickpeas and new potatoes recipe to add that extra crunch.

Ingredients

350g - 12oz gram flour
125ml - 4 fl oz very hot oil
15ml - 3tsp salt
6.25ml - 1¼tsp hanchora (rock salt)
water about 175ml - 6 fl oz or a little more to make the soft dough
oil for deep frying

Method

Heat the oil on the lowest setting ready for frying. Meanwhile heat the oil until almost boiling. Stir the hot oil into the sifted flour, and slowly and carefully incorporate all the flour.
Mix the salt, hanchora and warm water well, and add slowly to the flour, making a medium consistency of batter like dough.
Fill the sev machine with this dough choosing the template with the tiny holes.
Turn the handle and allow to drop in the hot oil rotating your hand to form a circle of sev in the oil.
When the oil has stopped bubbling then turn the whole circle over until the bubbling subsides. Lift out and drain well.
Carry on this same process until all the batter has been used up.
Cool and store in a glass bottle or air tight tin.

Fish Fritters

Ingredients

450g - 1lb old floury potatoes cut into small pieces
450g - 1lb white fish fillets
5 spring onions sliced finely
3 green chillies pounded
10ml - 2tsp garlic paste
5ml - 1tsp salt
fresh green coriander
15ml - 1tbsp medium or hot curry paste
2 beaten eggs
140g - 5oz fresh white breadcrumbs
vegetable oil for shallow frying
chutney to serve

Method

Cook the potatoes in a pan of boiling salted water and drain well. Return the potatoes to the pan and dry off until all the moisture has thoroughly evaporated, cool slightly then place in a food processor together with the fish, onions, chillies, garlic, salt and chopped fresh coriander.
Process until all the ingredients are finely chopped.
Into a bowl mix in 30ml - 2tbsp of beaten egg and the breadcrumbs. Reserve the remaining egg and breadcrumbs.
Divide this mixture into 8 and roll into a ball flattening slightly. Dip into the egg and breadcrumbs and fry on a medium heat in deep oil until golden brown. Remove with a slotted spoon and drain on kitchen towels.
Serve with chutney or relish of your choice.

Veg, Chicken & Spaghetti Spring Rolls

Indian cookery seems to have an inexhaustible store of savoury snacks. The savouries come in many varieties. Some are quite heavy while others are light on the stomach. Many Indian savouries are suitable as starters, elevenses or side dishes to be served with desserts and drinks or even at a picnic.
However, this recipe isn't truly Indian. The spices may be Asian, but the pastry is Chinese and the spaghetti Italian.
Combining these ingredients creates a delicious concoction. The making of this snack is quick and straightforward. Spring rolls offer considerable scope for experiment. Add or omit ingredients and spices as desired and be adventurous. Spring rolls - served on an attractive platter with various garnishes and decorations such as freshly sliced lemon, tomatoes and onions - are irresistible.

Ingredients

30ml - 2tbsp cooking oil
5ml - 1tsp cumin seeds
1 finely grated onion
225g - 8oz frozen vegetables
225g - 8oz chicken pieces
450g - 1lb frozen vegetables
salt to taste
a few green chillies
10ml - 2tsp garlic paste
¼ bunch fresh coriander
spring onions, pureed fine
10ml - 2tsp soy sauce
115g - 4oz chilli and garlic flavour spaghetti
55g - 2oz grated cheese
1 packet frozen Chinese or spring roll pastry

Method

Heat the oil and throw in the cumin seeds. When the spluttering has stopped, add the vegetables and washed and cubed chicken pieces. Add salt, garlic, green chilli paste and finely grated onion. Cook on medium heat, stirring occasionally until the moisture has evaporated. Meanwhile, boil the spaghetti as instructed on the packet. Drain and refresh with cold water. Leave to drain further.
When the vegetables and chicken have cooked and all water has evaporated, switch off and add the remaining ingredients.
Add the pasta and stir very well until all the ingredients have been fully incorporated.
The pastry, which has been left to defrost, should be separated individually. However, as each layer is very thin, you can use two layers for each roll. Place some mixture on one corner, fold in the other three corners like an envelope to cover the filling and roll tightly towards the last corner to make a roll. Glue together with a thin paste made from flour and water. Set aside until all rolls are complete. Deep fry the rolls on medium heat until just golden. Remove with a slotted spoon and arrange on a kitchen towel to remove excess oil.
Serve hot.

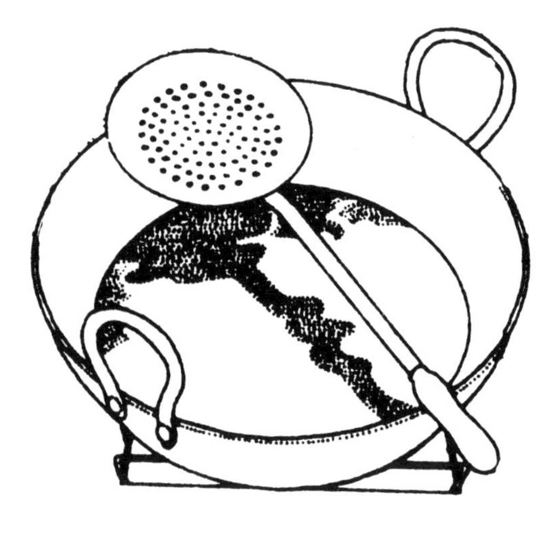

Tandoori Chicken

Chicken Makni served with Aromatic Rice

Tarkari

The general misconception is that the term 'curry' means an ingredient used in the preparation of Indian food. But, in fact, curry is a dish served with rice, bread or chappattis. Curry powder, which is sold in tins, is a mixture of dry ingredients and spices. Most Asian cooks do not use the pre-prepared powder available from supermarkets. Instead, they make up their own formula, adding or omitting various ingredients to make each dish unique.

Ingredients

125ml - 4 fl oz cooking oil
1 medium chicken cut into pieces
2 onions, finely sliced
3 large tomatoes, finely chopped
5ml - 1tsp garlic paste
15ml - 1tbsp ginger paste
10ml - 2tsp chilli powder
2.5ml - ½tsp cumin seeds
1.25ml - ¼tsp turmeric
20ml - 4tsp coriander powder
2 cinammon sticks
2 cardammon
5 whole black peppers
salt to taste
green dhania for garnish
garam masala

Method

Wash and drain chicken. Fry sliced onions, whole jeera, cardammon, black pepper and cinnamon until onion is golden brown. Add the chicken which has been marinated with garlic, ginger, chilli powder, turmeric and salt. Cook for 10 minutes on medium heat, stirring occasionally. When all the moisture from the chicken has evaporated, add the chopped tomatoes and cook for a further 10 minutes. Add 450ml - 16 fl oz of water and simmer until the curry is slightly thick.
Garnish with chopped green coriander and 2.5ml - ½ tsp garam masala (optional).
Serve with white rice (pilau) or chappattis.

Sweet & Sour Chicken

This recipe combines a sweet and sour flavour with a thick and creamy texture. Sweet and sour chicken is delicious served with coloured and tinted rice, naan or even couscous. It is so simple to make in very little time. The preparation time is minimal and the ingredients are simple. You will notice the absence of onion usually the base of a good curry. But the red chilli and tomato puree makes a very attractive addition and enhances the colour of the dish perfectly.
It is quite delicious served hot with a squeeze of lime and accompanied with tandoori naan or white pilau rice.

Ingredients

45ml - 3tbsp tomato puree
30ml - 2tbsp greek style yoghurt
2.5ml - ½tsp garam masala
5ml - 1tsp chilli powder
30ml - 2tbsp mango chutney
5ml - 1tsp garlic paste
5ml - 1tsp salt
7.5ml - 1½tsp sugar
60ml - 4tbsp corn oil
1 small chicken skinned and chopped small
150ml - 5 fl oz water
2 fresh green chillies chopped fine
30ml - 2tbsp chopped fresh coriander
30ml - 2tbsp single light cream

Method

Blend together the tomato puree, yoghurt, garam masala, chilli powder, garlic, mango chutney, salt and sugar. Mix well in a deep bowl. Heat oil in a deep non stick pan and lower the heat slightly and pour in the mixture. Bring to the boil and cook for about two minutes, stirring occasionally.
Add the chicken and stir until well coated. Add the water. Reduce heat, cover and cook until the chicken is tender. Finally add the fresh chillies, coriander and cream and cook for a few more minutes stirring occasionally.

Rogan Josh

Rogan means fat and josh literally means heat though figuratively it has come to mean intensity. Traditionally fatty meat on the bone was used to make rogan josh. The meat was traditionally cooked on a slow cooker in its own fat with a little extra added for flavour. However in these days of extra cholesterol-consciousness, we should avoid the excess use of fats and oil. Rogan josh derives its intensity from the lavish use of body heat-inducing spices such as the larger black cardommons and cloves.
The hallmark of the dish as cooked in Kashmir is the liberal use of the true Kashmiri red chilli. This has a mild flavour but imparts a fiery red colour.
This recipe is a creamy, well flavoured dish eaten with paratha or naan bread.

Ingredients

1kg - 2lb 4oz mixed lamb washed and drained
1kg - 2lb 4oz onion- very finely shredded
50ml - 2 fl oz cooking oil
6 large cardammons
4 small cardammon pods
a few cinammon sticks
few large cloves
12.5ml - 2½tsp salt
5ml - 1tsp turmeric
10ml - 2tsp ginger paste
10ml - 2tsp crushed garlic
1½ tins tomatoes pulverised
1 small tin tomato puree
10ml - 2tsp red chilli
20ml - 4tsp coriander powder powder
1 small green pepper/red pepper diced
a few whole green chillies
fresh green coriander chopped finely
1 bottle rogan josh mix

Method

Fry onions in oil until golden brown, add cardammon pods, cloves and cinammon sticks. Stir in the meat gently, adding the salt, turmeric, ginger and garlic. Stir well for a minute or so then cook on a very low heat. When all the moisture has evaporated add the tomatoes, tomato puree and other spices. Stir and cover cook on moderate heat until almost dry and tender. Add the peppers and whole chilli. Finally add the bottle of rogan josh mix stir again. Simmer for a while, switch off and add lots of fresh green coriander just before serving.

Chicken Makhni

With a creamy tomato base an interesting variation of chicken.

Ingredients

1kg - 2lb 4oz chicken
25g - 1oz butter
175g - 6oz tomato puree
5ml - 1tsp vegetable oil
5ml - 1tsp black cumin seeds
45ml - 3tbsp tandoori paste
10ml - 2tsp salt
175ml - 6 fl oz single cream
2 fresh green chillies thinly sliced

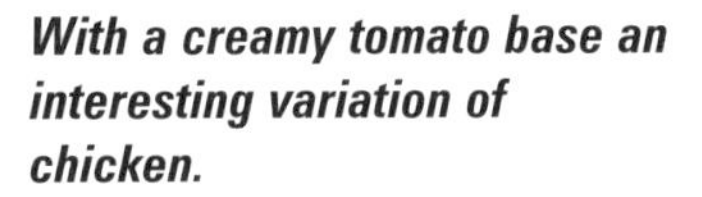

Method

Cut the chicken into 6 or 8 pieces, melt the butter and oil in a pan then stir in the cumin seeds and tomato puree, and tandoori paste.
Continue stirring until the mixture reaches boiling point and starts spluttering slightly.
Stir in the salt and chicken pieces, until all pieces are well coated for about 10 minutes.
Stir in the cream and continue cooking for a few minutes until blended and the chicken and sauce are hot.

Transfer to a serving dish and garnish with fresh chillies.

Creamed Coconut Chicken

Ingredients

1 kg - 2lb 4oz chicken
4 fresh green chillies
85g - 3oz creamed coconut
60ml vegetable oil
10 fresh karipulya leaves
280g - 10oz tomatoes very finely chopped
280g - 10oz onions grated
10ml - 2tsp salt
5ml - 1tsp turmeric
5ml - 1tsp garam masala
25g - 1oz tamarind pulp soaked in hot water and strained
30ml - 2tbsp tomato ketchup
freshly chopped coriander leaves to garnish

Paste

10ml - 2tsp ginger paste
10ml - 2tsp garlic paste
15ml - 1tbsp poppy seeds
3 whole red chillies
30ml - 2tbsp coriander seeds
30ml - 2tbsp cumin seeds
55g - 2oz desiccated coconut

Method

Soak the desiccated coconut for the paste in hot water for 30 minutes.
Toast the cumin, coriander and poppy seeds and chillies in a wok or a heavy pan. When lightly browned transfer into a small bowl. When cool grind until it forms a fine paste.
Cut the chicken into six pieces, slit the whole chillies and heat the oil in the same pan.
Add the grated onion and karipulya leaves and stir fry for a few minutes until they reach lightly golden shade.
Stir in the tomatoes and continue stirring until it dries.
Stir in the coconut paste, salt turmeric and garam masala and continue stirring on a medium heat until a dry masala is formed. Increase the heat to high and stir in the chicken and green chillies cooking at a lower heat. Stir occasionally for 5 minutes.
16 fl oz water should be poured and bring to the boil.
Uncovered cook the chicken and when boiling rapidly cover the pan and cook on low heat for 15 minutes until the juices run clear from the chicken and it is cooked.
Stir in the creamed coconut diluted tamarind pulp and tomato ketchup.
Return to boil and simmer stirring occasionally for five minutes.
Transfer to a casserole dish and garnish with chopped coriander and sliced green chilli.

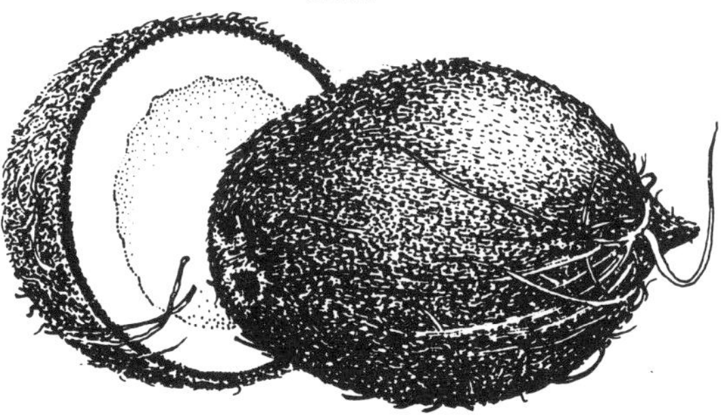

Chicken Extravaganza

Ingredients

1.5 kg - or approx 3lb chicken washed and scored
115g - 4oz butter
55g - 2oz raisins
175g - 6oz dried prunes, soaked stoned and sliced
175g - 6oz dried apricots soaked sliced and stoned
5ml - 1tsp ground cinammon
salt and freshly ground pepper to taste
5ml - 1tsp cumin powder

Method

Fry the onion in half of the butter for a few minutes until lightly golden, add the fruit and stir for a few minutes.
Season with salt and pepper and cumin powder.
Allow to cool. Pre heat the oven to gas mark 5 (190°C) and stuff the chicken with the mixture
Brush with remaining melted butter and rub liberally with salt and brown paper. Wrap tightly in cooking foil and bake in the hot oven. Open the foil after 50 minutes and cook for 45 minutes open until the skin is brown and crisp.

Lamb Kebabs

Meat has a high calorific value - mainly due to its saturated fat content. When buying meat, we need to take care to choose only the leanest meat and then trim away any visible fat before cooking.
It is advisable to eat meat in moderation to reduce consumption of fat as far as possible.
For lamb, the meat from the shoulder is the leanest, with very little visible fat.
Boneless meat is seldom used in Asian cookery. Kofte (kebabs or meatballs) are eaten as a starter, hors d'oeuvres, or as a main meal when accompanied by rice or naan bread.
Meatballs can be curried with a sauce based on tomatoes and onions, barbecued on a summer's evening, fried for snacks or picnics, served with spaghetti and, for the weight conscious, they can be grilled.
Meatballs are eaten throughout the world. They can be blended with different ingredients to create a variety of flavours. A common dish in the Middle East and Turkey where they are served with cooked rice, a platter of salad or fresh bread during a day's excursion to the islands. This is a common sight around the Mediterranean where captains light barbecues and crews serve tourists. The following recipe for kebabs can be cooked, ready to serve, in minimal time.

Ingredients

450g - 1lb lamb mince
2 medium sized onions, sliced
½ bunch green coriander
10ml - 2tsp garlic paste
5ml - 1tsp ginger paste
5ml - 1tsp turmeric
10ml - 2tsp fresh lemon juice
salt to taste
6 green chillies (adjust according to hotness desired)
15ml - 3tsp coriander powder
5ml - 1tsp garam masala

Method

Blend all the ingredients together, until you can just see pieces of onion. Take care not to make the onion pieces too small or the mixture will turn soggy.
Empty the contents on to a plate and make walnut-sized balls with either your hands dipped in flour or your palms dipped in cold water. This will ensure perfectly rounded kebabs and reduce stickiness, allowing for easier handling.
Make all the kebabs and place on a tray. Refrigerate for about 30 minutes until firm.
Heat oil for shallow frying. Fry the meatballs in small batches until golden brown.
Remove with a slotted spoon and drain on kitchen paper.
Serve with chutneys and fresh bread or naan with a healthy salad and lemon wedges.

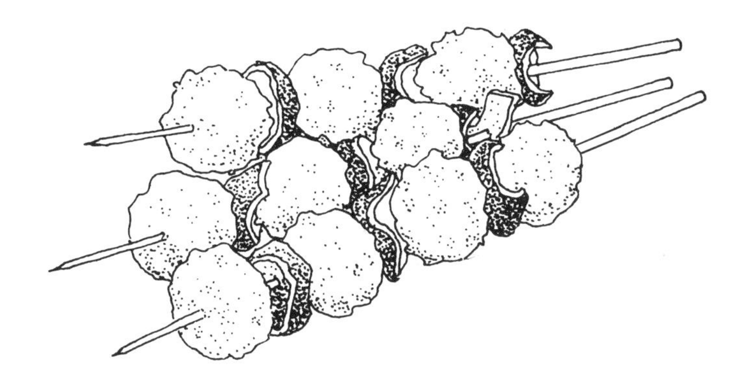

Kofte Curry

Here is an example of how you can be adventurous by interchanging complimentary recipes.

Marinate the kofte with the ingredients used in the Meatball recipe on page 33. (omit the potatoes.)

Make the curry by following the ingredients and method used for Tarkari on page 29. But replace the chicken with the marinated kofte.

Minced Lamb

Be sure to have the mince very lean with no fat and to mince it very fine.

Ingredients

700g - 1½lb finely minced lamb
3 cloves garlic
2 cinammon leaves
75ml - 2.5 fl oz oil
400g - 14oz onions, very finely chopped
1 cinammon stick
3 green cardammons
15ml - 1tbsp ginger paste
15ml - 1tbsp garlic paste
4 green chillies
1.25ml - ¼tsp turmeric
2.5ml - ½tsp cumin powder
10ml - 2tsp coriander powder
5ml - 1tsp garam masala
2 fresh tomatoes finely chopped
10ml - 2tsp salt
200g - 7oz frozen garden peas
115g - 4oz coriander leaves chopped finely

Method

Boil the mince in 450ml - 16 fl oz of water with one whole peeled garlic clove, and the cinammon stick for 10 minutes. This will cook the mince as well as removing the odour.
Strain away the water. Finely chop the garlic cloves.
Heat oil in cooking pot and fry the onions on low heat until golden brown. Add all the spices except the garam masala and mix well.
Add tomatoes and the garden peas, taste for salt adjusting if necessary.
When the moisture has evaporated, stir fry for a few more minutes and cook until tender.
Add the garam masala and the chopped coriander and give a final stir before serving.

Meatballs

Meatballs differ in flavour and shape from country to country. This recipe includes potatoes which have a flavour of their own as they are cooked with the juices from the meatballs. Absolutely delicious!

Ingredients

450g - 1lb lamb mince
10ml - 2tsp garlic paste
5ml - 1tsp ginger paste
5ml - 1tsp turmeric
juice of one fresh lemon
salt to taste
half bunch fresh coriander
half dozen sharp green chillies (adjust according to hotness required)
15ml - 3tsp coriander powder
5ml - 1tsp garam masala

3 large potatoes cut into medium-sized pieces
5ml - 1tsp salt
2.5ml - ½tsp turmeric
5ml - 1tsp red chilli powder
vegetable oil

Method

Blend all the ingredients well. Marinate for a few hours if possible. In a large wok heat 125ml - 4 fl oz vegetable oil. Add the potatoes to which the salt, turmeric and chilli has been mixed. Lower the heat and cover.
Meanwhile, make round meatballs from the mince mixture.Then add to potatoes, covering the potatoes with the meatballs, and close with a tight-fitting lid.
The potatoes will cook from their own juices. When both the meatballs and potatoes are cooked, make the heat high to reduce the volume of liquid. Place in an ovenproof dish and brown in a hot oven before serving.
This dish tastes delicious if served with thick rice flour rotla, chappattis.

Spicy Lamb Burgers

Eating habits are changing and today's younger generation seem to have a great desire to experience an authentic taste in a form associated with Western cuisine.
In accommodating a hectic working life and ensuring that the family table is set daily with freshly made food, preparing in minimum time is a skill in itself.
Some dishes can be partly prepared in the morning and finished in the evening just before the meal is served.
Other foods can be marinated overnight ready to oven bake or roast the following day.
Many foods can be prepared, frozen and fried within minutes and with suitable accompaniments such as chips, vegetables etc. can be turned into a meal in itself.
It's simply a matter of juggling around schedules during the normal working week and to make a firm decision to sit around a table and eat and talk together at that specific time of day. In doing so advocating the traditional family values.
Obviously, the more the merrier, but there is no doubt that there is something tremendously significant about the gift of food.
It needs some reverence so that even if you are eating alone you should treat the meal as something special.
It's at the dining table that confidences are exchanged and family life makes a contribution, and is it among the remains of a family meal or when you're elbow-deep in peelings that you pause for a moment and think: "What is life really about?"
Food not only reinforces ethnic ties but also allows for Western cuisine to have an influence on Asian cookery.
Here is a recipe for lamb burgers (lamb kebabs) fried, filled in pitta bread or sesame seed buns.
It is the addition of spices that makes the burger a successful step forward when trying to entice the palates of both the younger and older generations.

Ingredients

650g - 1lb 8oz lean minced lamb
1 large onion
1 fresh tomato
½ bunch fresh green coriander
some fresh shallots, finely chopped
fresh lemon
6 green chillies or adjust according to hotness required
5ml - 1tsp garlic paste
5ml - 1tsp ginger paste
10ml - 2tsp salt
2.5ml - ½tsp turmeric
20ml - 4tsp coriander powder
2.5ml - ½tsp garam masala
2.5ml - ½tsp soy sauce
2 slices fresh white bread
30ml - 2tbsp gram flour
oil for frying

Method

Wash and drain or squeeze dry the mince.
Finely chop the onion, tomato, fresh coriander, and shallots. Pound finely the green chillies. Remove the edges of the bread and place in a blender to make fine bread- crumbs.
Sift the gram flour and put all the ingredients into a blender with the juice of half a fresh lemon and blend for almost a minute-not more. All the ingredients should be well incorporated with each other and the mixture is now ready for use.
You may need to moisten your hands with cold water for easier handling. First form into a ball, then flatten into the size required on the palm of your hand gently into a circle. Carry on with the rest of the mixture. (These can now be frozen for later use if required). Fry in a frying pan, turning occasionally until browned and cooked.
Drain on kitchen paper. Make a salad, fill the pitta bread or burger bun, add sauces, relishes, chutney or mint sauce, mayonnaise, and savour the flavour!

Green Peppers With Khima

'Capsicum annuum', more commonly known as peppers, are natives of South America, the Mediterranean and tropical countries.
Peppers are very rich in vitamin C and there are more than 200 varieties.
Ripe red peppers are sweeter and mellower in flavour than the green varieties.
Yellow peppers are closer in flavour to the red variety. In a box of green peppers there may be some that are beginning to turn yellow or red. These are in the process of ripening. They will eventually turn red, though, as they are off the plant, they may wrinkle as they mature.
Avoid peppers that are wrinkled or those with brown patches when choosing any variety or colour.
Peppers should always be smooth and sleek with a glossy brightness. Green and red peppers, and even yellow varieties, are readily available. They are great assets in everyday diet for both hot and cold dishes.
Peppers with the core and seeds removed and with the flesh chopped in tiny pieces can be added in small quantities to soups and casseroles to enhance the flavour. They are also very much part of Chinese stir-fried dishes.
A pepper is an invaluable crispy ingredient for salads and cold dishes.
It is not necessary to skin the vegetable, as doing so removes most of its valuable properties.
Peppers also have medicinal properties. In Brazil doctors who specialise in peppers and their use are known as pimentologos.
Their claims have some basis in truth because capsicums are rich in vitamins.
Peppers in moderation aid the flow of gastric juices and promote digestion.
They provide some of the most popular spices available.
Chillies form the backbone of many of world's cuisines.
Many chefs have made it the hallmark of their cooking.
Peppers and pepper products are now commonplace on the Western table.

Ingredients

4 medium sized green peppers
2 medium sized onions, finely sliced
2 medium sized new potatoes, peeled and cubed
2 fresh tomatoes, finely sliced
500g - 1lb 2oz chicken mince, washed and drained
30ml - 2tbsp olive oil
85g - 3oz butter
chopped green coriander
6 green chillies (adjust according to hotness required)
7.5ml - 1½tsp salt
2.5ml - ½tsp turmeric
20ml - 4tsp coriander powder
2tsp garlic paste
10ml - 2tsp ginger paste
2.5ml - ½tsp garam masala

Method

Fry the onions in olive oil and butter until soft and yellow.
Add the mince to which the coriander, chillies, salt, turmeric, garlic, ginger and garam masala have been added. Knead thoroughly.
Cook on medium heat until almost dry. Add the potatoes and tomatoes and mix well.
Cover for a few minutes, mixing occasionally until the potatoes are cooked. Take off the heat.
Wash the peppers, remove the seeds and cores and fill with the prepared stuffing.
Return to heat with a few tablespoons of water. Cover with cooking foil and a lid and cook on very low heat.
Open after about 20 minutes.
Turn the peppers carefully, cover again and cook gently until the peppers are tender.
Serve with freshly made chappattis, pitta bread or tandoori naan.

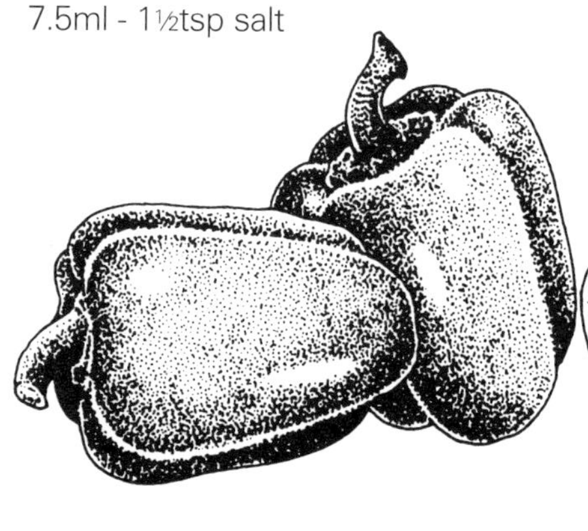
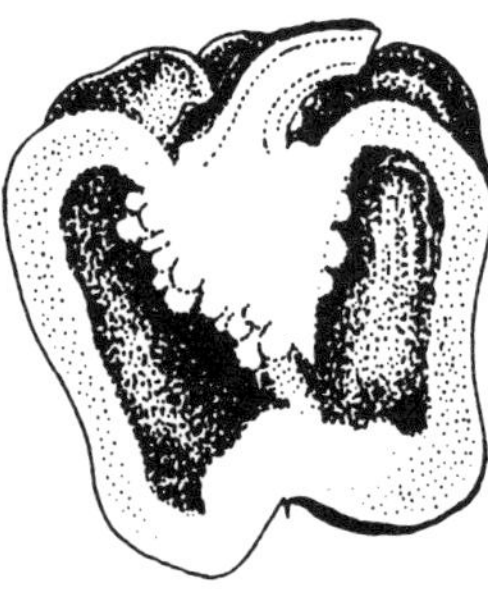

Marinated Lamb Chops

Meat is often cut and smeared with marinades before being cooked. A marinade tenderises the meat and infuses it with all the flavours and aromas of its many ingredients.
The meat can then be grilled, roasted or cooked on the stove, while retaining the taste of all the seasonings.
Most dry roast meat dishes include garam masala. This spice combination varies from home to home though the name is constant.
Garam means hot and masala means spices. Thus, the spices in garam masala were traditionally those which 'heated' the body according to the ayurvedic system of medicine.
The spices all happened to be highly aromatic as well. Commercial mixtures tend to cut down on expensive cardammon and fill up the mixture with cheaper spices. It is always advisable to make your own.

Generally, garam masala is used as a pep to spice up sprinkled towards the end of cooking to retain aroma. But it is also included in marinades to deliver double the benefit Lamb chops can be served as a starter or as part of the main meal if not covered in breadcrumbs and fried.

Ingredients

10 lamb chops
2.5ml - ½tsp garam masala
45ml - 3tbsp oil
Juice of one fresh lemon
10ml - 2tsp ginger paste
10ml - 2tsp garlic paste
10ml - 2tsp green chillies, pounded
20ml - 4tsp coriander powder
5ml - 1tsp red chilli powder
5ml - 1tsp tandoori powder
5ml - 1tsp salt (or to taste)
½ bunch fresh coriander, very finely chopped
breadcrumbs
1 egg

Method

Wash and drain the meat well. Make a paste with all the ingredients except thc egg and the breadcrumbs. Smear the chops well with the paste and leave to marinate overnight or for a few hours.
Place the chops in a heavy-based frying pan and cook on slow heat until tender.
Remove from the heat and cool.
Beat the egg, adding a little salt and pepper. Dip the chops firstly in the egg and then in the breadcrumbs.
Fry on medium heat for a while, then drain. Arrange on a serving dish with salad and lemon wedges.

Tandoori Cutlets

Ingredients

10 lamb cutlets, washed and drained
45ml - 3tbsp tandoori paste
30ml - 2tbsp lemon juice
5ml - 1tsp coriander powder
5ml - 1tsp cumin powder
15ml - 1tbsp fresh chopped coriander
5ml - 1tsp turmeric
280g - 10oz yoghurt

Method

Marinate the cutlets in the ingredients which have been well blended together.

Place the cutlets in a deep bowl and turn spooning the excess marinade over the cutlets ensuring they are completely covered. Cover with cling film and leave overnight to absorb the flavour.
In the morning remove each one with a slotted spoon and reserve the excess liquid. Cook on a barbecue or in a pre heated oven turning a couple of times and brushing occasionally with melted butter.

Mint sauce

100g - 3½ oz yoghurt
5ml - 1tsp cumin powder
15ml - 1tbsp mint sauce
5ml - 1tsp green chilli paste
5ml - 1tsp garlic paste
melted butter for basting

Method

Mix all the ingredients well and serve with the cutlets.

Turkey with Herbs & Spices

Gone are the days when only the rich ate turkey and then it was only once a year. Today's turkeys are such good value for money that they could take the place of traditional Sunday roast.
Turkey was the favourite food for festive occasions and, because it was rare, it was looked upon as a delicacy. Therefore, it became associated with special days such as Christmas or Thanksgiving.
However, nowadays, even non-Christians look forward to feasting on turkey during the festive holidays.
And it is quite common to see signs in Islamic halal butchers requesting orders for turkeys. With the addition of spices and herbs, turkeys are easily adapted to Asian or Oriental cuisine. And they do not necessarily have to be stuffed. By observing a few rules a turkey can be roasted to produce crispy golden skin and moist tender flesh.

Ingredients

1 medium weight turkey

Marinade

Mix together the following
15ml - 3tsp salt
7.5ml - 1½tsp turmeric
120ml - 8tbsp coriander powder
15ml - 1tbsp garlic paste
30ml - 2tbsp ginger paste
45ml - 3tbsp red chilli powder
30ml - 2tbsp clear honey
juice of 1 lemon and 2 limes
½ bunch fresh chopped coriander
75ml - 5tbsp cooking oil
5ml - 1tsp garam masala

Method

Clean and wash the turkey well. Score the flesh with a sharp knife. Marinate the turkey overnight in the masala and, in the morning place the turkey on to a roasting tin with all the marinade.
Dot with butter and cook for approximately two and a half hours on gas mark 3 (170°C) or until the turkey is cooked.
Remove from the oven and let the roast stand for about 15 minutes to allow the flesh to set and to make the carving easier.
Serve with vegetables and roast potatoes or chips.
Alternatively, serve with rice or chappattis.
This recipe is for a medium sized turkey to feed a fairly large family. Cooking times will have to be adjusted according to the size of the bird.
Another method, which requires a shorter oven time, is pot roasting.
Either chop the turkey into reasonably sized pieces or leave whole. Marinated overnight, the turkey can be cooked on a slow stove until most of the moisture has evaporated and it is almost cooked.
Finish off by transferring to a roasting dish and placing in an oven until golden brown and cooked.

Dry Pan Roast Chicken

Ingredients

1 chicken approx lkg - 2lb
350g - 12oz onion roughly chopped
115g - 4oz fresh coconut peeled and grated
125ml - 4 fl oz vegetable oil
7.5ml - 1½tsp cumin seeds
8 black pepper corns
8 cloves
15ml - 1tbsp fennel seeds
15ml - 1tbsp coriander seeds
60ml - 4tbsp chopped fresh coriander
lemon wedges to serve

Method

Heat the oil in a heavy based pan, add the cumin seeds, peppercorns, cloves, fennel, coriander seeds and when the seeds have stopped spluttering stir in the onion. Stir fry until lightly golden, add the coconut and continue stirring until the mixture starts to change into a golden colour. Turn off the heat and allow to cool slightly.
Blend very fine in a processor.
Meanwhile wash and score the chicken deeply and place in the pan with the paste and mix thoroughly coating the chicken well. Stir fry on a medium heat for a few more minutes incorporating all the spices into the chicken and then cover and simmer until the chicken is thoroughly cooked. Stir in half the chopped coriander and mix well. Just before serving transfer to a platter and garnish with the remaining coriander and lemon wedges.

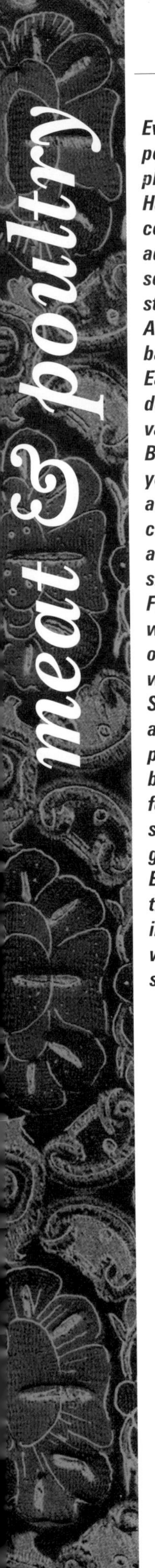

Every year more and more people are discovering the pleasures of outdoor eating. Hardware stores, garden centres and chain stores are adding more and more sophisticated ranges to their stock.

An enormous range of barbecues is available today. Each model having different design detail that cater for various types of cooking.

But, whatever your purchase, you will almost certainly need accessories such as fuel or coal, fire-lighters, cooking foil, a basting brush, tongs and skewers for kebabs.

For fish you can buy broilers which overcome the problem of turning a partly cooked fish without causing it to break.

So, why barbecue? What is the attraction? Barbecuing is popular throughout the world because it cooks top quality food in the best way possible, sealing in all natural juices and goodness.

Barbecuing cooks food up to the point that is just right for individual preferences, whether tastes are plain or spicy. Recipes can be made up by anyone using favourite marinades and seasonings. Thus, each person can add his or her own signature to the craft of barbecue cooking.

Barbecuing is also an informal way of entertaining family and friends.

It creates an atmosphere of relaxed informality, breaking down barriers and involving everyone in the preparation, be it cooking, carrying or serving.

Barbecuing is a challenge to serve up food to perfection. It gives the cook a tremendous feeling of satisfaction when he or she succeeds.

Diet, calories, nutrition, reducing cholesterol and losing weight, at the same time as retaining an interest in food, play important roles in barbecuing.

Meat grilled over hot charcoal tastes delicious and removes the calories that are normally added by frying.

You can barbecue almost anything. Green peppers, fish, tomatoes stuffed and wrapped in foil, vegetable burgers and corn on the cob, as well as other vegetables, each have a unique flavour when cooked on an open fire.

With modern barbecue equipment it is not difficult to produce a wide and delicious variety of gourmet cooking that is normally associated with the kitchen, oven or microwave.

And all that fresh outdoor air laden with the aroma of sizzling food works wonders on the appetite. But perhaps the most welcome benefit of barbecuing is that it releases the regular cook (still the housewife in most households) from domestic and culinary chores.

There is almost no washing up to do if paper plates and cups are used. Food can be marinated and prepared in advance and stored in the refrigerator.

The housewife may not have to cook at all if her husband or a friend takes charge. Usually all those involved in the cooking process enjoy themselves.

Barbecuing is a cheerful, relaxed and fun way of entertaining that people around the globe have known for centuries.

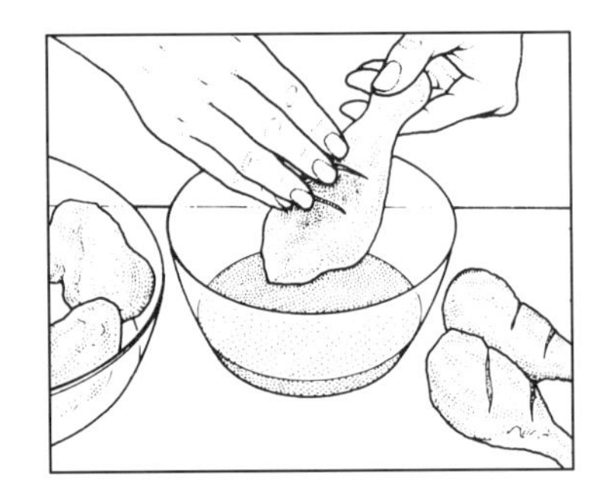

Barbecue Marinade

Here is the perfect marinade for that special summer barbecue:

Marinade

10ml - 2tsp salt
30ml - 6tsp red chilli powder
30ml - 6tsp coriander powder
5ml - 1tsp turmeric
½ bunch chopped fresh coriander
10ml - 2tsp garlic paste
20ml - 4tsp ginger paste
25ml - 5tsp yoghurt
10ml - 2tsp ground tandoori powder (not paste)
oil to make paste

Baste

Gently heat the juice of one fresh lemon with 10ml - 2tsp honey.

Method

Marinate the meat (you can use any meat but chicken and lamb are particularly popular). Double or treble the recipe according to the quantity of meat (washed and drained). Cook on the barbecue and, just before the meat is ready to serve, baste it using the honey and lemon mixture. This gives the meat a tangy flavour and a shiny, glazed appearance.
Serve with fresh salad and drinks.

Creamy Cashew Chicken

Ingredients

225g - 8oz chicken cubes
ghee for frying
15ml - 1tbsp plain flour
10ml - 2tsp pepper
salt to taste
55g - 2oz cashew nuts (soaked for a couple of hours in a little water)
115g - 4oz cauliflower florets
115g - 4oz pineapple cut into 2.5cm strips
1 onion grated
10ml - 2tsp tomato puree
2.5ml - ½tsp garam masala

Marinade

30ml - 2tbsp curd
2.5ml - ½tsp ginger paste
2.5ml - ½tsp garlic paste
5ml - 1tsp pulverised green chilli
2.5ml - ½tsp salt
2.5ml - ½tsp garam masala
10ml - 2tsp chopped coriander leaves
10 fried cashew nuts

Method

Heat 2.5ml - ½tsp ghee in a pan add the flour and pepper and stir briskly. Add the salt and gradually add a little water and stir continuously to obtain a smooth paste. Cook for 3 minutes and cool. Mix all the ingredients well for the marinade and coat the chicken well. Leave in a cool place for 3 hours and then fry in ghee till tender and golden brown. Grind the cashew nuts to a fine paste and stir fry the cauliflower florets in a little ghee till golden brown and remove with a slotted spoon. Sprinkle the ¼tsp salt to the pineapple strips and steam for 7 minutes. Heat 30ml - 2tbsp ghee in a pan and saute the onion till glossy and transparent. Add the pepper and tomato puree, garam masala and salt. Stir fry until the ghee rises to the top add the cashew nut paste and add 2½ cups of water, stir well, add the chicken and florets when the gravy starts to boil cover the pan and simmer on a low heat for 20 mins add the pineapple and white sauce and stir gently for 5 minutes. Serve garnished with chopped coriander leaves and whole cashew nuts.

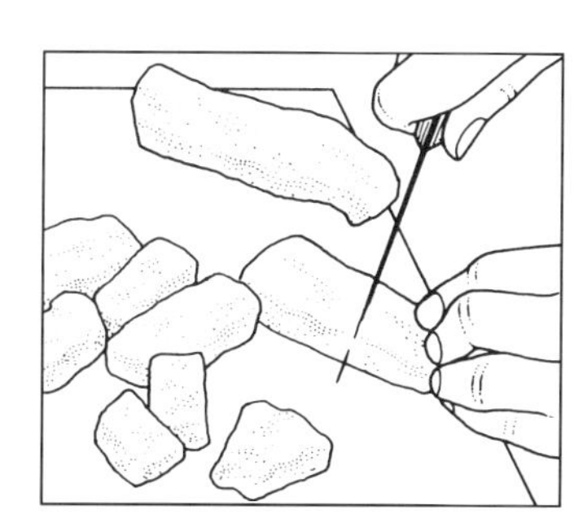

Jahangiri Murgh

This dish is so simple to make and is a valuable contribution to a dinner party or when a guest has arrived.
It is a speciality of Jahangir from the times of the Moghul Empire.

Ingredients

8 chicken drumsticks
90ml - 6tbsp yoghurt
15ml - 1tbsp ginger paste
15ml - 1tbsp garlic paste
60ml - 4tbsp ghee
2 medium onions finely chopped
2 tomatoes chopped
10ml - 2tsp coriander powder
5ml - 1tsp cumin powder
5ml - 1tsp chilli powder
2.5ml - ½tsp turmeric
30ml - 2tbsp cashew nuts
salt to taste
5ml - 1tsp garam masala
500ml - 18 fl oz boiling water
few slivered green chillies and freshly chopped coriander to garnish

Method

Wash the drumsticks and score all over.
Mix the yoghurt and ginger/garlic paste and smear all over the chicken.
Leave to marinate for a few hours.
Heat the ghee and fry the onion until a rich golden colour
Add tomatoes, nuts chilli powder, coriander, cumin and turmeric. Continue stirring until the ghee separates.
Add the marinated chicken and salt to taste. Stir frequently cooking on a low heat. When the moisture has evaporated add the water and simmer on a low heat until the chicken is cooked.
Sprinkle the garam masala and coriander and fresh green chilli to garnish serve with hot naan or puri.

Kholapur Chicken

This dish originates from Kholapur in Southern India. Although the people of that region eat their meals with plenty of chillies in this recipe the chilli has been reduced, however it is up to the individuals taste to add more if required.

Ingredients

1.5kg - 3lb 5oz chicken, cut into small pieces
1 large onion coarsely chopped
45ml - 3tbsp garlic paste
15ml - 1tbsp ginger paste
10ml - 2tsp coriander powder
5ml - 1tsp cumin powder
15ml - 3tsp chilli powder
1 small tin chopped tomatoes
2.5ml - ½tsp salt
6 whole green chillies
5ml - 1tsp garam masala
45ml - 3tbsp cooking oil
45ml - 3tbsp ghee
30ml - 2tbsp chopped fresh coriander

Method

In a processor, blend the onion, garlic, ginger adding a little water. Heat the oil and fry these ingredients for a few minutes, then add turmeric, coriander powder, cumin, and chilli powder adjusting the heat to low and fry for 5 minutes, stirring frequently.
Add half of the tomatoes and stir in well carry on cooking for 3 minutes.
Add the chicken and stir well ensuring the chicken is well mixed in with the spices then add the remaining tomato and salt.
Bring to the boil and simmer until the chicken is cooked.
Finally add the coriander, green chillies and garam masala and after 5 minutes turn off.
This dish is now ready for serving.

Curried Meatballs - Kofte

Andaman Prawn Curry

Fish - rich in vitamins, oil and protein - has always played a prominent role in the Asian diet. It offers as much variety as meat. Many different types are available ranging from rich, strongly flavoured, oily fish like herring, mackerel, trout and salmon to more subtle and delicate white fish such as cod and tilapia.

Fish combines great nutritional value with the added advantage of being easy to digest. And, in the case of white fish, it has low fat content.

All these qualities make fish the perfect choice for a meal, especially for slimmers or the health conscious.

Then there is the luxury of shellfish in all its exotic forms and flavours, for example jinga (prawns).

A huge variety of shellfish imported from various countries around the world, including India and Bangladesh, is available in Britain today.

Indeed, Bengalis have a great passion for fish. No meal would be complete without it. Salted fish is also very popular. And perhaps the most widely known dried fish is bhumla (Bombay Duck or Mumbai Duck).

In fact, this is not a duck at all but a long, narrow fish that is plentiful in the sea surrounding Bombay, hence the name Bombay Duck.

Bhumla are usually served in small pieces as an accompaniment. They are salty and strongly flavoured. Their texture is crisp and crumbly when fried but they are just as delicious grilled.

Fish can be cooked in many ways. It can be grilled, fried or curried. Also, tandoori fish is becoming increasingly popular.

Remember the following hints when buying fresh fish:

- *Look for firm red gills that are hard to open. Make sure the fins are not flabby.*
- *Fresh fish should have all scales in place, a moist body, bright eyes and firm flesh.*
- *White fish should not have a blue tint.*
- *There should be no unusual smell.*
- *It is best to cook fish on the day it is purchased.*

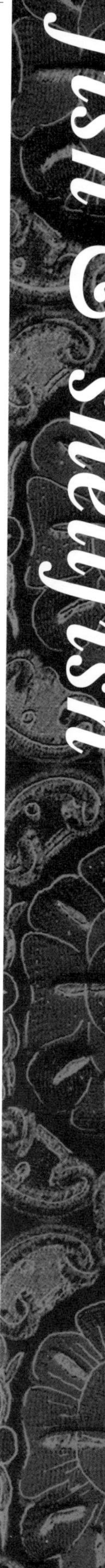

Fish in Yoghurt Sauce

Ingredients

700g - 1½ lb white fish, sliced or whole but scored
10ml - 2tsp crushed garlic
7.5ml - 1½tsp salt
10ml - 2tsp fresh ground red chillies
6ml - ¾tsp turmeric
10ml - 2tsp coriander powder
5ml - 1tsp cumin powder
15ml - 1tbsp finely grated fresh coconut
60ml - 4tbsp oil or margarine
225ml - 8 fl oz yoghurt
1 onion, grated
2 green chillies
chopped fresh coriander leaves for garnish
karipulya (curry leaves)

Method

Mix the crushed garlic, salt, fresh ground red chillies, turmeric, coriander powder, cumin powder and finely grated fresh coconut with a tablespoon of the yoghurt.
Smear the washed fish with half of the paste (not forgetting the insides of the fish and the slits if the fish has been kept whole).
Fry onions in oil. Add the curry leaves when the onions are nearly golden.
Add the rest of the marinade to the onion and mix for a few minutes.
Then add the rest of yoghurt and the fish.
Simmer until cooked (in about 30 minutes).
Alternatively, place the fish in an ovenproof dish, pour the fried onion and braised marinade over, cover with foil and bake in a moderate oven for 30-40 minutes.
To garnish, sprinkle chopped coriander and serve with spicy rice or aromatic rice or chappattis and pickles.

Poppy Seeds & Prawns

Poppy seeds are available in two colours, white and blue-grey.
The white variety, known as khus khus or posta in Bengal, comes from the ripe seeds of the poppy plant papaver somniferum.
The cream-white seeds used in India are much smaller than the blue-grey variety sprinkled on cakes and breads in Europe and America although they are very similar in flavour.
Like sesame seeds, poppy seeds are indispensable in many Bengali dishes.
Powdered, wet, ground or whole, the seeds are routinely baked, dry roasted or fried to bring out their dormant nutty flavour.
Perhaps the most outstanding use of poppy seeds is as a thickener for sauces and gravies.
Powdered poppy seeds combined with crushed spices add a wonderful flavour to many dishes.
Today, they are available from most supermarkets. Like nuts and seeds with a high oil content, they are best stored in a cool place.
To be adventurous you could substitute the prawns with chicken, white vegetables or even cassava cubes. The variety is almost endless.

Ingredients

55g - 2oz white poppy seeds soaked overnight in hot water
2 medium onions, finely sliced
1 large tin tomatoes
6 green chillies
225g - 8oz prawns - cleaned, washed and marinated overnight in garlic, salt and turmeric
½ bunch finely chopped fresh green coriander
5ml - 1tsp ginger paste
10ml - 2tsp garlic paste
10ml - 2tsp coriander powder
7.5ml - 1½tsp salt
2.5ml - ½tsp turmeric
vegetable cooking oil

Method

Carefully rinse the poppy seeds in a fine sieve and drain. Fry the marinated prawns in some oil until almost cooked. Remove with a slotted spoon.
Add the onion and saute in the oil until just golden.
Meanwhile, pulverise the tomatoes, green chillies and poppy seeds in a blender or liquidiser until the mixture is very smooth.
If time allows it is better to pound the seeds with a pestle and mortar for better results.
Add the tomato mixture to the onions and stir until almost all the liquid has evaporated.
Then add the prawns and cook gently for a while and switch off. Garnish with lots of chopped coriander.

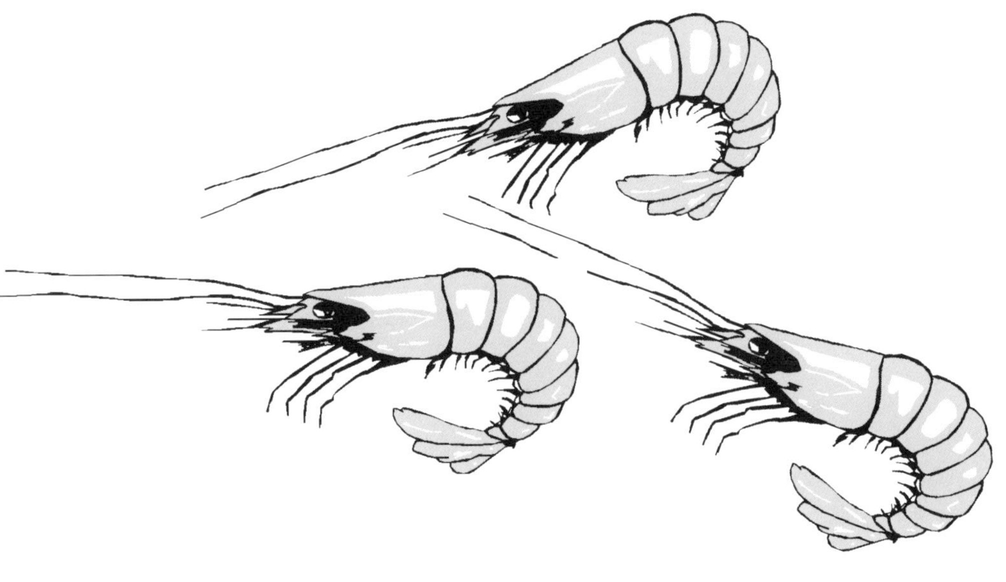

Prawn Curry Special

Fish is considered 'food for the brain' and is eaten and enjoyed by almost everyone.
Indeed, people from the state of Tamil Nadu in Southern India look to the sea for their livelihood.
A profusion of fresh fish and seafood is available right on their doorstep - both from the sea and from five large rivers.
Today, fish from Madras is exported all over the world and fishing plays an important part in the state's economy.
The wealth of seafood includes mussels and shrimps, plump prawns (large blue veined, tiger or pink) and glorious lobsters.
The sweetness of succulent prawns is drawn out by cooking with coconuts or tomatoes.
But fish prepared with tamarind, a harmony of sweet and spice with a little contrast of sourness, is delicious.
The best prawns for this recipe are tiger or king prawns but you must remember to de-vein them.
The Andaman Islands in the Indian Ocean are officially part of the Tamil Nadu state.
This recipe originates from the islands where prawns are cooked in a creamy coconut sauce with a little chilli for some fire and a touch of tamarind.

Ingredients

450g - 1lb king or tiger prawns
2 medium onions
2 cloves garlic
3 green chillies
25g - 1oz tamarind pulp
cooking oil
a few karipulya leaves
5ml - 1tsp mustard seeds
5ml - 1tsp cumin seeds
60ml - 4tbsp coconut milk
5ml - 1tsp chilli powder
2.5ml - ½tsp turmeric
salt to taste

Method

Peel and chop the onion and garlic finely. Slice the green chillies lengthways.
Infuse the tamarind in 60ml - 4 tbsp of boiling water for 5 minutes.
Squeeze the pulp, strain and set aside the liquid.
Heat a little oil in a pan. Add the karipulya leaves, onion and garlic. Fry until the onions are soft.
Then add the mustard and cumin seeds. Mix in the tamarind juice, coconut milk, chilli powder, turmeric, salt and sliced green chillies.
Add the prawns and simmer gently until they are cooked.
Serve with rice, roti or naan.

Baked Fish

Ingredients

600g - 1½lb fish fillet
55g - 2oz chopped onions
700ml - 25 fl oz thick tomato puree
2 green peppers deseeded and chopped
salt and freshly ground black pepper to taste
5ml - 1tsp chilli powder
10ml - 2tsp garlic paste
25g - 1oz coriander chopped fine
45ml - 3tbsp olive oil
juice of half a lemon

Method

Cut the fish into 4cm wide strips. Pre heat the oven to gas mark 4 (180°C), grease a medium sized casserole dish. Mix onion, tomato puree and chopped peppers well. Place 1/3 in a layer in the casserole and lay half the fish strips over the top. Season with salt pepper and chilli powder, repeat the layers and mix the last third of tomatoes and peppers with the garlic and coriander and spread on the top layer. Gently press the layers down, mix the oil and lemon juice and pour over and bake for an hour, basting with a little oil. Serve with lemon wedges and crusted bread.

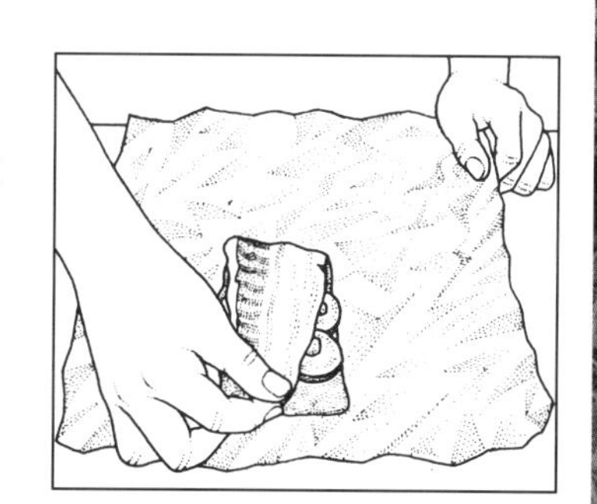

Deep Fried Fish

Ingredients

450g - 1lb white fish
85g - 3oz onion
10ml - 2tsp garlic paste
10ml - 2tsp ginger paste
55g - 2oz yoghurt
5ml - 1tsp chilli powder
2.5ml - ½tsp turmeric
5ml - 1tsp salt
2.5ml - ½tsp garam masala
vegetable oil for deep frying
chopped fresh coriander and lemon wedged to garnish

Method

Cut the fish into 1cm thick slices and roughly chop the onion. Put the onion, garlic and ginger into a food processor until a smooth paste forms.
Mix this onion paste with the yoghurt and chilli powder, turmeric, salt and garam masala and stir until well blended.
Add the fish stirring gently to coat all the pieces in the marinade.
Cover the bowl and chill in the fridge for a few hours.
Use a slotted spoon to remove the fish from the marinade and place on a rack allowing excess marinade to drain off.
Heat the oil in a large heavy based sauce pan or wok over a high heat and fry in the hot oil lower the heat to medium and fry till crisp and golden.
Place on kitchen towels to drain excess fat. Garnish and serve.

Madras Fish

The marinating of this fish is a combination of vinegar and lime juice which eliminates the strong fishy smell, and the grinding of the coconut without adding water improves the taste.
The gravy is pungent and thick and goes very well with yellow rice.

Ingredients

900g - 2lb fish steaks, skinned
juice of a lime
10ml - 2tsp cider vinegar
225g - 8oz fresh grated coconut
15ml - 1tbsp ginger paste
30ml - 2tbsp garlic paste
450g - 1lb tomatoes chopped
30ml - 6tsp poppy seeds pounded
10ml - 2tsp tamarind pulp
75ml - 2.5 fl oz cooking oil
1.25ml - ¼tsp mustard seeds
350g - 12oz onion chopped finely
12 karipulya leaves
10ml - 2tsp coriander powder
2.5ml - ½tsp turmeric
10ml - 2tsp chilli powder
salt to taste
2.5ml - ½tsp fennel seeds and 2.5ml - ½tsp cumin seeds pounded together

Method

Marinate the fish with lime juice and vinegar for 30 minutes, put the grated coconut into a blender with the ginger, garlic tomatoes and poppy seeds, process well for 30 seconds.
Soak the tamarind in 250ml - 8 fl oz of hot water.
Heat oil in a shallow fry pan and add the mustard seeds. When they start to splutter add the onions and fry till lightly golden brown. Then add the curry leaves, followed shortly by the coriander, turmeric and chilli powder. Stir fry for a minute.
Add the coconut mixture and stir fry then add the tamarind water some salt and 450ml - 16 fl oz of water. Bring to the boil and simmer for 3 minutes. Gently lay the fish in the pan turning the heat very low. Sprinkle with the mixture of fennel seeds and cumin seeds and cook until the fish is tender.

Fish Kofte

Ingredients

450g - 1lb fish
55g - 2oz margarine
egg for binding
5ml - 1tsp garlic paste
1 slice of white bread
1 onion grated
15ml - 1tbsp chopped spring onions
15ml - 1tbsp chopped fresh coriander
15ml - 1tbsp chopped fresh mint
5ml - 1tsp salt
10ml - 2tsp green chillies pounded
2 large grated tomatoes
juice of fresh lime
fresh coriander for garnishing

Roast Spices

2.5ml - ½tsp of coriander seeds
2.5ml - ½tsp cumin seeds
3 red dry chillies
5ml - 1tsp sesame seeds
2.5 - ½tsp sea salt

Method

Steam the fish till cooked and flake of all the flesh. Add all the remaining ingredients and form into fishballs. Fry in the oil and then prepare the curry. In a dry pan roast the spices and pound all together. Remove the meatballs after they are dry and in the same pan add the spices and braise for a few minutes and replace the koftas and add the grated tomatoes. Simmer until the masala is well mixed with the fishball, sprinkle with fresh lime juice and fresh coriander and serve with roti or rice.

Creamy Cod Slices

Try this recipe served with either an assortment of rices or rotis and you will cook it time and time again. Cooked in a rich and colourful tomato and coconut sauce with minimum effort.

Ingredients

4 steaks of white fish, either cod or coley
1 onion chopped finely
10ml - 2tsp garlic paste
½ red and ½ green pepper seeded and chopped
5ml - 1tsp coriander powder
5ml - 1tsp cumin powder
5ml - 1tsp turmeric
2.5ml - ½tsp garam masala
400g - 14oz can of chopped tomatoes
150ml - ½pt of coconut milk
30ml - 2tbsp chopped fresh coriander or parsley
salt and pepper to taste

Method

Heat the oil in a frying pan and add the fish steaks to which salt and pepper has been rubbed.
Fry on a medium heat until golden brown on both sides. Then add the onion, garlic paste and green chillies, the chopped red and green peppers and other spices. Mix well and stir for a couple of minutes on a low heat. Add the tinned tomatoes and bring to the boil on a high heat, then reduce the heat again and continue stirring until all the moisture had evaporated. Simmer gently for a few minutes. Carefully place the fish slices into the pan and spoon some sauce over the top.
Continue simmering until the fish is thoroughly cooked.
In a small pan pour the coconut milk and sprinkle the fresh coriander and when warmed through gently spoon over the fish just before serving.

Tamarind Fish

This fish has a delicious and tangy taste to it with the addition of tamarind. The flavour seems to improve by cooking in a claypot rather then aluminium as the lemon juice is acidic. A stainless steel pan or pot would be ideal too.

Ingredients

450g - 1lb firm white fish, cod would be ideal
5 ml - 1tsp salt
15ml - 3tsp red chilli powder
10ml - 2tsp coriander powder
45g - 1¼oz tamarind
1 large onion
3 cloves garlic
2 tomatoes
45ml - 3tbsp cooking oil
15ml - 1tbsp fenugreek seeds
15ml - 2tsp tomato puree
15ml - 3oz fresh coriander leaves
5ml - 1tsp garam masala
30ml - 2 tbsp lemon juice

Method

Wash and dry the fish that has already been cleaned. Sprinkle liberally with salt and slice into 2" pieces.
Make a paste with the chilli powder, coriander powder, garlic and tomato puree and lemon juice.
Infuse the tamarind in 350g - 450ml boiling water for 10 minutes then strain through a sieve and reserve the liquid.
Peel and coarsely chop the onion, roughly chop the tomatoes.
Fry the onions in the oil until soft and glossy, add the fenugreek and fry slowly until a warm aroma is released then add the paste which has already been prepared. Fry for 2 mins and slowly add the fish, turn over once gently after a few minutes then add the tomatoes, simmer gently for about 15 minutes then gently pour in the tamarind, lower the heat and cover the pan with a lid and let the moisture evaporate.
Turn off the heat and add the chopped coriander leaves.

Crunchy Plaice

Ingredients

3 small onions
10ml - 2tsp garlic paste
10ml - 2tsp green chilli paste
450g - 1lb fish pomfret or plaice
5ml - 1tsp salt
2.5ml - ½tsp turmeric
15ml - 3tsp sesame seeds
60ml - 4tbsp cooking oil
1 fresh lime
60ml - 4tbsp fresh coriander
6 karipulya leaves

Method

Marinate the fish a couple of hours before cooking.
Peel the onions, garlic and with the chilli paste and karipulya leaves. Process altogether until fine.
Clean and wash the fish and marinate evenly with salt, turmeric which has been mixed in the paste for a couple of hours.
Roast the sesame seeds in a heavy based non stick pan taking care not to burn.
Shallow fry the marinated fish in oil until it is crisp.
Garnish with roasted sesame seeds and slices of lime and fresh coriander. Serve immediately on a bed of spicy rice or with paratha.

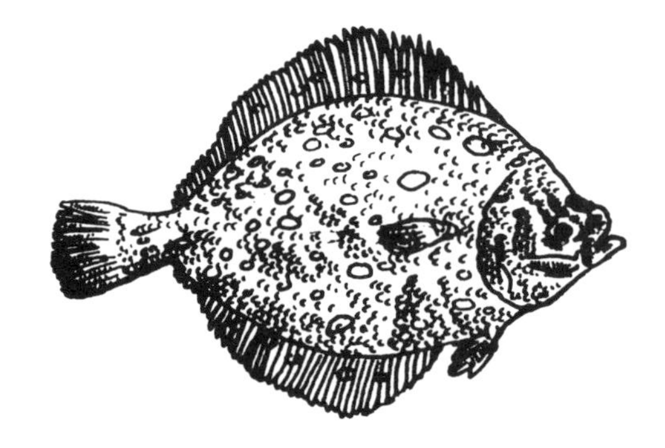

Chori & Methi Bhaji

Aubergine & Potato Fry

Aubergine & Potato Fry

Different varieties of aubergine are available from the market these days.
The humble aubergine - also called brinjal, egg plant or vengra - is a native of India although it is now grown in other part of the world, including Kenya and Uganda.
Aubergines come in various shades of pink, purple and green and white as well as in assorted shapes and sizes.
The flesh inside is soft and white with tiny edible seeds.
Like other vegetables, the aubergine has almost endless uses. It can be stuffed, curried, roasted, cooked as fritters or sauteed.
The most common aubergines are the long purple ones.
These are ideal for this recipe.
Aubergines are rich in Vitamin C and dietary fibre. Cooked with potatoes, as in this recipe, they make a delicious meal.
Boiled new potatoes or tinned potatoes can be used.

Ingredients

1 large purple aubergine (about 350g - 12oz)
225g - 8oz potatoes, boiled in their skins, cooled & peeled
45ml - 3tbsp corn or vegetable oil
2.5ml - ½tsp black mustard seeds
2.5ml - ½tsp onion seeds
1 medium onion, finely chopped
10ml - 2tsp ginger paste
10ml - 2tsp garlic paste
5ml - 1tsp ground fennel
10ml - 2tsp cumin powder
10ml - 2tsp chilli powder
5ml - 1tsp salt (or to taste)
a few baby sweetcorn
425ml - 15 fl oz warm water
55g - 2oz tomato puree
5ml - 1tsp garam masala
45ml - 3tbsp chopped coriander

Method

Quarter the aubergine and cut into 5cm - 2 inch lengths. Soak in a large bowl of water with 10ml - 2 tsp salt for 30 minutes. Drain and rinse. Cut the potatoes into 5cm - 2 inch cubes. Preheat a wok pan over the medium heat for a few seconds, then add the oil.
When hot, add the mustard seeds. As soon as they pop, add the onion seeds, then the finely chopped onion.
Stir-fry for 6-8 minutes or until the onion begins to change colour. Add the ginger and garlic. Stir for a minute.
Add the ground fennel and cumin, turmeric and chilli powder. Stir-fry for 20 seconds. Then add the salt, warm water, aubergine, baby corn and tomato puree.
Bring to boil and reduce heat to medium. Cook uncovered for 10 minutes, stirring frequently to ensure the aubergine cooks evenly. At the start of cooking the aubergine will float but, once it soaks up the liquid, it will sink and cook quite fast.
When this has happened add the potatoes and cook for a few minutes.
Sprinkle the garam masala and stir in the fresh coriander to complete the dish.
Serve with masala roti or naan bread for a truly authentic meal.

Balti Masoor Dhal

A quick lentil to prepare is this red lentils which makes a useful change from meat and fish at the same time providing essential proteins.

Ingredients

225g - 8oz split skinless lentil (masoor dhal)
600ml water
5ml - 1tsp salt
2.5ml - ½tsp red chilli powder
1.25ml - ¼tsp turmeric
3 cloves garlic peeled and thinly sliced
85gm - 3oz chopped fresh tomato
30ml - 2tbsp oil
1 fresh green chilli
30ml - 2tbsp chopped fresh coriander

Method

Wash dhal in a sieve until water runs clear. Soak for 30 minute, drain.
Put the dhal into a pan and add enough water to cover the dhal.
Add the salt, chilli powder, turmeric, garlic and tomatoes.
Bring to the boil and simmer and cover for 10 minutes until dhal is cooked but has retained its shape.
Heat the oil in a pan and add the remaining garlic slices when sizzling and golden brown, remove from the heat.
Pour onto the dhal but do not stir in.
Garnish with fresh chillies slices and coriander.
Serve straight from the Karai with fresh chappatti or naan.

Spicy Dasheen

The tropical plant dasheen is grown in many hot regions of the world. In some areas it forms a major part of the everyday diet, providing no less than four foods in one plant.
Dasheen offers huge leaves known as elephant ears, leaf stalks and runners, tender young shoots and starchy tubers.
The word dasheen, the plant's most common name- is thought to originate from 'da china' or 'de chine'. In Gujarati it is called commodia kun.
Like the onion and potato the dasheen has been eaten for centuries. This vegetable is popular all over the world.
We must give credit to those who first sorted the edible plants from ones that are almost edible, inedible and extremely poisonous.
The dasheen has a truly wonderful taste and texture. It has slightly pink flesh on the inside and is slightly sticky. The vegetable is washed in lemon juice to remove the stickiness.

Ingredients

2 dasheens
2 medium onions
1 medium green pepper
4 large fresh tomatoes
30ml - 2tbsp tomato puree
30ml - 2tbsp garlic paste
6 green chillies
30ml - 2tbsp coriander powder
10ml - 2tsp salt
2.5ml - ½tsp turmeric
vegetable oil for cooking
½ bunch fresh coriander
1 fresh lemon

Method

Peel and cube the dasheen. Rinse, sprinkle with juice of half a lemon and leave aside.
Fry the finely sliced onions in a little oil until slightly golden.
Chop the tomatoes and green pepper and pulverise the garlic and green chillies.
Add the salt, coriander powder, tomato puree and turmeric. Mix everything in the frying pan.
Stir well, mixing all the ingredients. Reduce heat, cover and allow to cook slowly.
Wash the dasheen in cool water and drain. When most of the moisture in the pan has evaporated and the tomatoes have become mushy, add the vegetable, mixing all the ingredients well. Cover and simmer.
After a few minutes add 125ml - 4 fl oz water and simmer until cooked.
Switch off the cooker. Add the washed and finely chopped coriander and squeeze in the remaining half of the lemon.
The dish is now ready to serve.

Falafel

Ingredients

450g - 1lb dried broad beans
6 spring onions finely chopped
3 cloves garlic crushed
5ml - 1tsp cumin powder
10ml - 2tsp fresh coriander finely chopped
20ml - 4tsp freshly chopped parsley
salt and cayenne pepper to taste
oil for deep frying

Method

Soak the beans overnight in plenty of cold water.
Drain the next day and skin them. Grind them in a food processor, add all the ingredients together and blend to a smooth consistency.
Leave to stand for 15 minutes and chill in a fridge. This will enable easier handling of the paste.
Moisten your hands with water and make round balls flattening slightly and deep fry a few at a time. Serve with lemon wedges.

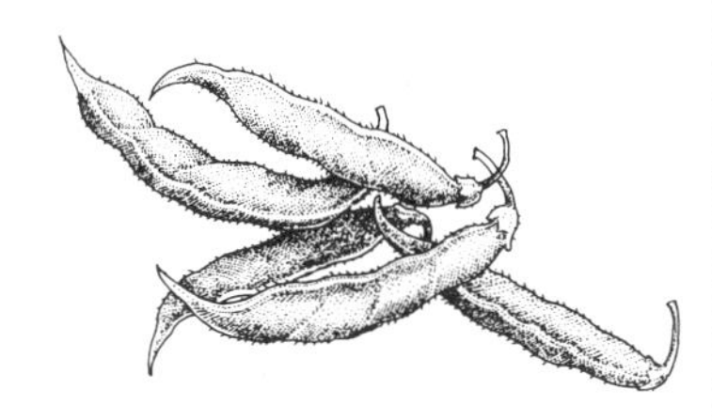

Vegetable Lasagne

Pasta has become an international favourite in most households and most kitchens would probably have a few packets of assorted pastas.
The non-Italians tend to make a complete meal of pasta and salad, but in Italy pasta would be eaten as a first course, followed by meat, fish or vegetable dishes.
Although I was convinced that pasta was only worth eating in Italian restaurants, after experimenting and adapting various recipes suitable for satisfying the tastebuds of the family, I became truly enthusiastic in preparing different methods.
Food should be prepared with care and affection, good quality, fresh seasonal produce is essential and the natural flavour of the dish should not be masked with complicated sauces.
The culinary tradition of Italy is based on vegetables, cereals, fish and olive oil. Many health-giving nutritive and medicinal qualities are attributed to the oil in its raw state- a healthy way forward which appeals to most tastes.
Indeed all recipes are versatile, adapting them to prevailing circumstances. If you cannot find a certain ingredient, improvise and use what is available. The dish will taste different, but it will have your own personal touch. Happy cooking. Buon appetito.

Ingredients

1 large aubergine
1 medium courgette
30ml - 2tbsp olive oil
2 small onions
2 medium red potatoes, peeled & chopped
425g - 15oz can chopped tomatoes
5 green chillies
1 small green pepper
2 eggs
225ml - 8 fl oz milk
30ml - 2tbsp yoghurt
grated cheese
a few karipulya leaves
2.5ml - ½tsp cumin seeds
5ml - 1tsp ginger paste
5ml - 1tsp garlic paste
2.5ml - ½tsp turmeric
10ml - 2tsp salt or to taste
freshly ground pepper to taste
lasagne sheets (no-cook variety)

Method

Wash and slice the aubergine and courgettes, put in a colander and sprinkle with salt. Leave to drain for about 30 minutes. Rinse and pat dry.
Meanwhile, preheat the oven to gas mark 5 (190°C/375F).
Heat the oil in a pan, add the karipulya leaves and cumin seeds. When this has stopped crackling add the onions and saute until soft.
Add the courgettes and aubergines and potatoes, and stir-fry for a few minutes.
Add the tomatoes, spices and pounded green chillies and 125ml - 4 fl oz of water.
Cover and simmer for 20 minutes.
Add more water until the mixture is fairly liquid, as the 'no-cook' lasagne absorbs a lot of liquid. In a suitable oven dish spread a layer of half of the vegetable mixture, followed by a layer of lasagne, then repeat. Beat the eggs and milk in a bowl, stir in the yoghurt and pour over the lasagne. Sprinkle generously with cheese, and bake for approximately 40 minutes.

Mattar Paneer

Paneer is a delicious fresh soft cheese frequently used in Asian cookery. It can be made at home but a ready made paneer is widely available at most grocery stores.

Ingredients

2 onions chopped
30ml - 2tbsp garlic paste
5ml - 1tsp garam masala
5ml - 1tsp turmeric
5ml - 1tsp chilli powder
500g - 1lb 2oz frozen peas
200g - 7oz can chopped tomatoes
225ml - 8 fl oz water
salt and black pepper
30ml - 2tbsp fresh coriander
100ml - 3½ fl oz vegetable oil
450g - 1lb paneer

Method

Heat oil in a large frying pan. Add the cubed paneer and fry till golden on both sides. Drain on paper towels. Pour away some of the oil used for frying leaving about 60ml - 4tbsp in the pan add the onion and all the spices and fry gently for about 5 minutes. Add the tomatoes and stir again adding the peas and the water. Cover and simmer for 10 minutes until everything is cooked. Finally add the fried paneer and stir in well. Sprinkle with the fresh coriander and serve with hot chappattis.

Palak Paneer

Ingredients

30ml - 2tbsp ghee
1 onion sliced
1 garlic clove crushed
2 dried red chillies
5ml - 1tsp turmeric
450g - 1lb potatoes cubed
425g - 15oz can of tomatoes chopped and drained
150ml - 5 fl oz water
450g - 1lb paneer cubed
225g - 8oz fresh chopped spinach
5ml - 1tsp garam masala
30ml - 2tbsp chopped fresh coriander
15ml - 1tbsp chopped fresh parsley
salt and pepper to taste

Method

Cook the onion in the ghee until soft. Add the garlic and chilli and cook for a few minutes.
Add the turmeric, salt, potatoes tomatoes and water and cover and boil.
Simmer until the potatoes are cooked thoroughly.
Stir in the spinach, cheese cubes, garam masala, coriander and parsley. Season to taste.
Simmer for a while longer and serve with naan or paratha.

Mixed Vegetables & Turnip

We all come across a time during a hectic week, when we haven't had the time to prepare a meal in the morning before leaving for work.
And, when it's been one of those days when meetings went on longer than they should have, the phone never stopped ringing and all the inquiries came at once, you're pushed to get the dinner on the table.
But it's too late to worry now, even though you are rushing home, knowing that the children are due to return from school in 45 minutes.
With all their "hard work" and running around, they never seem to tire of saying: "We're starving!" So, what do you do?
Picking up some baby aubergines, a can or two from the pantry and grabbing the spice tin, you begin to prepare a filling and nourishing meal.
One of the ingredients in this quick recipe is turnip - a very 'English vegetable'.
The humble turnip comes from the tuber family.
Many varieties are available, from flat and round to long.
The white-fleshed tubers or roots sometimes come with a coloured head. Young turnips are particularly mild in flavour.
Varieties are grown in Japan, China, Italy, France and Britain.
Turnips have excellent nutritional value. They are high in calcium and in vitamin C.
But it was the Italian white redheaded variety that particularly captured my attention.
This variety is round with purple-red streaks down the side. It is pretty and nutritious too. While the food is simmering merrily on the cooker you can set the table and look organised.
You know any moment the front door is going to burst open and the school bags will be flung on the floor and there'll be shouts of "Mum, what have you cooked today? I'm starving".
There you are, looking perfectly calm and composed, smiling affectionately and saying: "Yes, thank you. I had a nice day too!"

Ingredients

45ml - 3tbsp sunflower oil
1 onion
4 green chillies, pounded
1 turnip
4 baby aubergines
425g - 15oz can lima beans
425g - 15oz can chopped tomatoes
2.5ml - ½tsp salt (adjust according to taste)
Freshly ground pepper
15ml - 1tbsp coriander powder
5ml - 1tsp garlic paste
5ml - 1tsp ginger paste
fresh coriander leaves

Method

Heat the oil in a pan. Add finely chopped onions until softened. Take care not to brown.
Add the tomatoes with all the spices and chillies. Stir on medium heat until almost dry.
Add the peeled and diced turnip and the washed and diced aubergines. Stir and cover. Simmer for about 10 minutes.
Meanwhile, wash the beans in a colander and drain. Wash and chop the fresh coriander for garnish.
Stir the vegetables occasionally. If necessary add 50ml - 2 fl oz of water to help the turnip to cook.
Finally, add the beans and stir lightly.
Garnish with chopped coriander.
This is a quick dish that can be served with white rice, hot chappattis or even pitta bread.

Chori & Methi

Pulses, beans and lentils, along with rice and vegetables, form a very important part of Asian and Oriental cuisine. Rich in protein and carbohydrates, they play a vital role in the diet of most vegetarians.
A large selection of pulses, dried beans and peas is available from Asian grocery stores.
High Street supermarkets and health stores also now stock a good variety.
Pulses of a single type can be bought in two forms- whole or split.
Varieties such as chick peas or chana dhal (split chickpeas) can be ground into a thick paste, made into dumplings and fried.
Pulses, in the form of flour, can be made into a batter to coat vegetables, which are then fried to make savoury teatime treats.

Ingredients

175g - 6oz black-eyed beans (pre-soaked overnight, then boiled until tender)
1 medium onion, sliced
5 green chillies
2 large tomatoes chopped very finely
1 potato, peeled and cubed
60ml - 4tbsp vegetable oil
½ bunch methi bhaji (fenugreek herbs) cleaned, washed and chopped. Fresh palak (spinach) can be used instead
Salt to taste
2.5ml - ½tsp turmeric
15ml - 1tbsp ginger-garlic paste
30ml - 2tbsp coriander powder
lemon juice

Method

Fry onion in oil until slightly golden. Add the potatoes and fry for a few minutes. When nearly cooked add tomatoes and all the spices.
Cover and simmer on low heat, stirring occasionally.
When potatoes are cooked and tomatoes have reduced in volume, add the pre-boiled beans and methi bhaji and cook for a further 10 minutes on low heat, stirring now and again.
Sprinkle with fresh lemon juice just before serving.
Serve with chappattis, pickles and papadums.

Stuffed Aubergines

Ingredients

450g - 1lb aubergines
5 green chillies
2.5ml - ½tsp salt or to taste
30ml - 2tbsp lime juice
2 medium tomatoes grated
¼ cup vegetable oil
2.5ml - ½tsp cumin seeds
5ml - 1tsp cumin powder
10ml - 2tsp garlic paste
2.5ml - ½tsp turmeric
10ml - 2tsp coriander powder
30ml - 2tbsp chopped fresh coriander
1 grated onion
1 peeled potato, cubed small

Optional

225g - 8oz baby prawns

Method

Wash the aubergines and slit from the bottom end but take care to leave the stem intact. They should be just able to open out with ease. To the lemon juice add all the ingredients and mix well. Stuff the aubergines with the filling as full as possible and gently lay down in a non stick fry pan. Cover with a lid tightly and cook on the lowest setting for about 15 minutes. Open the lid and very carefully with a large slotted spoon turn over on the other side. Cover and cook again until most of the moisture has evaporated and the filling is cooked. Serve with rice flour rotlas.

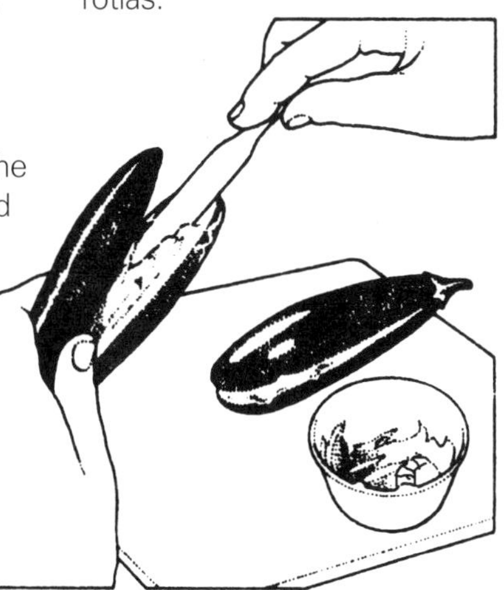

The cassava, a vegetable from the tuber family, originated from South America and was brought to Spain in the 16th century.
From Spain it was taken to Africa, and from Africa onto Asia where it was immensely popular by the 19th century.
The two types of cassava, sweet and bitter, are now planted over 37 million acres worldwide and 20 million acres in Africa alone.
The tender leaves and stem tops of the shrub are eaten as vegetables. The important part of the vegetable is the heavily swollen tuber, rich in starch. This can be ground into flour (tapioca) by a process of grating, rinsing, soaking and drying.
The cassava, also known as mogo, is a thick, irregularly shaped root, brownish and rich in starch, with excellent nutritional values, rich in vitamins A and C, and containing plenty of protein, calcium and iron.
The tubers should be peeled and boiled, then cut into chips or chunks and cooked in the desired way.
There are frozen cassavas already peeled and ready to boil which are widely available in supermarkets and are just as nutritious.
The cassava is one of those versatile vegetables, which can be used to make savoury dishes, chips and even a dessert.
In this recipe it is used in conjunction with chicken to make a curry, which is a rather filling and satisfying meal. Vegetarians may like to substitute soya 'meat' or quorn, which is a meat substitute.

Ingredients

1 medium chicken, cut into small pieces
1 packet of frozen cassava
2 medium onions finely sliced
425g - 15oz can of tomatoes
60ml - 4tbsp vegetable oil
5ml - 1tsp ginger paste
10ml - 2tsp garlic paste
2.5ml - ½tsp turmeric
6 fresh green chillies (or more if preferred hotter)
salt to taste
15ml - 3tsp coriander powder
2.5ml - ½tsp cumin powder
juice of 1 lemon
½ bunch fresh coriander leaves (for garnishing)
few sticks of cinnamon, few pods of cardammon and 6 pepper corns
few karipulya leaves

Method

Boil the cassavas according to the instructions on the pack. When tender, drain, allow cooling, removing any visible veins and cutting into 2.5cm - 1 inch cubes.
In a pan, warm the oil and on a very low heat fry the finely sliced onions together with the karipulya leaves, cinnamon sticks, cardammon pods and peppercorns. Meanwhile wash and cut the chicken into small pieces, marinate with the ginger/garlic paste, salt, turmeric, pounded green chillies, coriander and cumin powder. Mix well and leave aside.
Liquidise the tomatoes and when the onions are slightly golden add the tomatoes and stir gently over a medium heat. When almost dry and oil is visible on the top, it is possible to liquidise this onion and tomato mixture for a smoother curry. It is not necessary and the marinated chicken should now be added, stirred in and left to cook until the chicken is tender.
Cover and stir occasionally. When cooked, add the prepared cassava and 225g - 8 fl oz and simmer until the gravy is thick enough.
Switch off and add the lemon juice and chopped coriander just before serving.

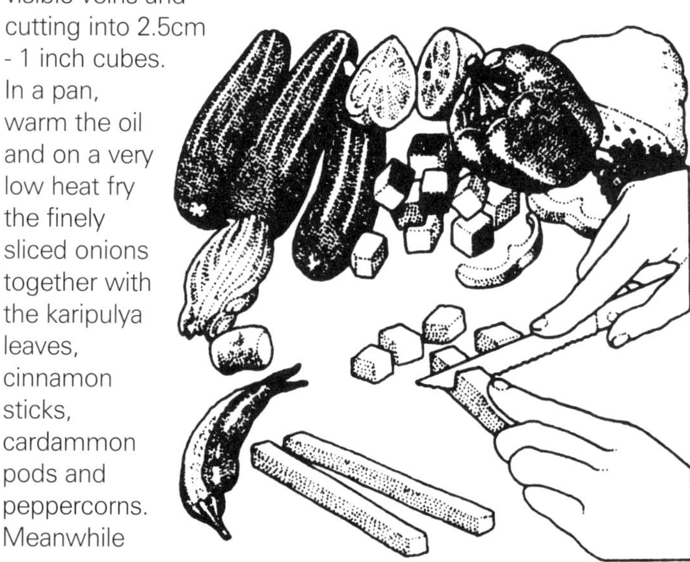

Okra & Dhal

The range of vegetables available today is exhilarating for the adventurous cook. More and more cornershops and supermarket offer Middle Eastern and Asian producc. This vegetarian cornucopia, along with other influences, travel abroad, interest in health and nutrition and the inspiration provided by some outstanding restaurants - has encouraged many cooks to leaf through cookery books for new ideas.
And, far from making your meals seem routine, flavour enhancers can bring out subordinate tastes. Aromatics like cumin, fennel and onion seeds, curry leaves, coriander, and asafoetida, positively add to the taste experience. Properly cooked fresh vegetables are the basis of healthy eating. They are bursting with energy-giving vitamins, minerals and carbohydrates. But wilted produce is never a bargain. Vegetables start loosing flavour and nutrients the moment they are picked. So thc sooner they are cooked the more you are assured of tenderness, taste and nutrition. Today's recipe is strictly vegetarian. It has an interesting combination of lentils and vegetables.

Ingredients

115g - 4oz of yellow lentils (tuwar dhal)
45ml - 3tbsp corn oil
2.5ml - ½tsp cumin seeds
2.5ml - ½tsp fennel seeds
½ thinly sliced onion
2.5ml - ½tsp garlic paste
5ml - 1tsp ginger paste
2.5ml - ½tsp red chilli powder
1.25ml - ¼tsp coriander powder
1 green unripe mango, peeled and sliced
½ packet frozen sliced okra
salt to taste
30ml - 2tbsp chopped fresh coriander
1 fresh tomato sliced

Method

Wash the lentils and boil in water until soft, taking care not to make them mushy. Drain and leave to cool. Heat oil in a deep skillet and fry seeds until they have popped. Add onion and fry until golden brown. Lower heat and add ginger/garlic paste, chilli powder and coriander powder.
Throw in the mango slices and okra stirring well. Stir fry for a few minutes until okra is cooked. Finally add the lentils, cook for a further five minutes. Serve hot with chappattis and papadums.

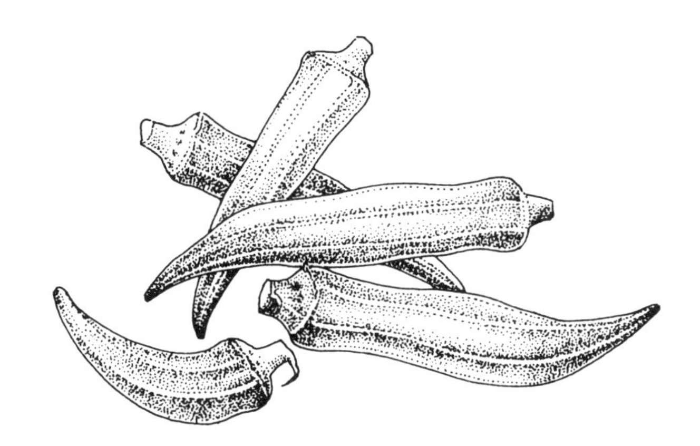

Ginger Paak

The hakims of India often sell recipes for palatable herbs which help towards the recovery for prevention from certain ailments. Some of these recipes have acquired the status of family heirlooms, and many have earned a valuable place in the cooking repertoires of many Asian grandmothers. The making of such foods seem to be a dying art, as the modern trend is to take pills and capsules rather then natural remedies. But ginger is universally recognised as a most natural and effective root vegetable for curing and preventing colds, coughs, and other related illnesses.
Herbal medicine practitioners advise that, at the onset of winter, a few fresh slices should be added to your daily tea, which also imparts a unique flavour. Ginger paak is extremely nourishing as it contains ingredients that are high in vitamins and iron. The amount of ginger used in this recipe can be altered according to the individuals preference of the strength of the ginger. This recipe is quite mild and you will find that children will eat it readily and reach for more.

Ingredients

225g - 8oz ginger, washed, peeled and processed finely
450g - 1lb jaggary
100g - 3½oz coarsely ground almonds
175g - 6oz dessicated coconut
60g - 2oz khus khus (poppy seeds)
55g - 2oz charoli
225g - 8oz ghee

For decoration

85g - 3oz fresh coconut sliced thinly
sesame seeds, roasted
ground pistachio nuts, to be sprinkled on top at the last minute

Method

Warm ghee and jaggery on low heat when the jaggery has melted, add the ginger and braise very slowly until it has browned and is almost dry in texture. Add the other ingredients and blend well, stirring and incorporating everything for almost 15 minutes on the lowest heat. Turn out into a greased tray and spread out evenly about 5mm - ¼ inch in depth. Decorate and cut into diamond shapes with a sharp knife until it sets.
Eat a slice a day at breakfast time to ward of coughs and colds.

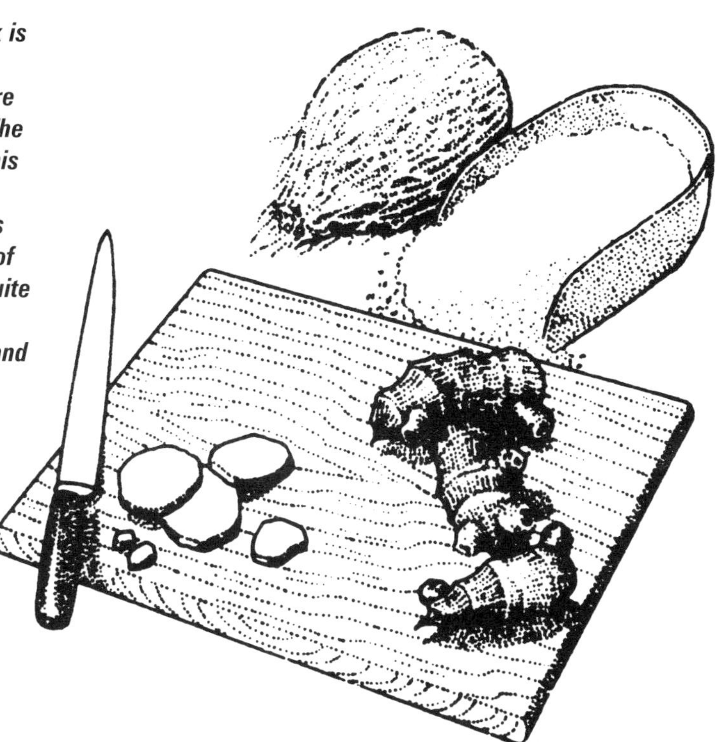

Chindru

- an old favourite

For centuries, dried peas and beans have been recognised as protein staple foods, they have played an important role in culinary tradition in India. The generic name for all members of the dried pea and bean family, and the dishes made from them is dhal. The repertoire of dhal dishes is so vast that you can make different recipes each day of the week if you wish. The dhals can be made into soups, sauces, stews, fried savouries and crispy pancakes. The imaginative and experienced cook can select a dhal dish to suit any meal, from breakfast to dinner. You can vary the dishes according to season- warm and hearty for the winter and light and refreshing for the summer. Nutritionists say all dried beans are rich in iron and vitamin B and include substantial amount of protein. This recipe is a traditional dish that appears to be dying out in the present generation, yet it is nourishing, filling and delicious.

Although the name is a little peculiar the older generations who created it certainly know its value.

Ingredients

½ packet frozen pigeon peas
115g - 4oz rice flour
30ml - 2tbsp melted ghee
5ml - 1tsp salt
2.5ml - ½tsp sugar
to serve - boiled milk and enough sugar to taste

Method

Boil the pigeon peas in plenty of water for approximately 5 minutes or as stated on the packet.
Meanwhile sift the rice flour. Add salt, rub in the ghee until it resemble fine breadcrumbs. With some water taken from the pan of boiling peas, make a pliable dough- not too soft but firm enough to make shapes.
Take a little dough and roll into a marble sized dough then flatten very slightly. It should not be round but almost oblong.
When all the pieces are done, leave about 4 in a basin, and together with the 2.5ml - ½tsp sugar, add all but the four to the peas.
Then boil. Thin down the remaining 4 with water to make a paste. Add this to the pan. Boil and when thick enough switch off the heat.

To serve, boil some milk in a pan, serve out some of the mixture and pour the hot milk over the top add sugar to taste. The chindru is now ready to eat.

Bhagale Polo

Whether visitors are family, friends or strangers, gracious hospitality is typical of the Middle East.
The cuisine of Iran, both with meat and vegetables, is rich because of the abundance of good products available in the area.
Polo, similar to pilau, is traditional to Iran. In fact, the art of cooking rice almost certainly began in Persia.
Polo has given birth to many similar Middle Eastern rice dishes. The rice cooker, an invaluable appliance, is a familiar sight in Iranian kitchens. These cookers make rice to perfection to the desired level of crispness.
Persian cuisine, with its distinctive style, has evolved over many centuries.
Fresh herbs are used imaginatively in the Middle East. Some are familiar and widely available in Britain.
A wander around any Middle Eastern soukh or bazaar reveals heaps of colourful and fragrant herbs, which are used in handfuls rather than spoonfuls.
A typical Persian herb garden includes a collection of basil, dill, chervil, coriander, mint, chives and melokia - the list is almost endless.
Polo is a popular dish. It contains dill, a fresh and refreshing herb whose aniseed flavour enhances meat and vegetable rice dishes.

Ingredients

450g - 1lb lamb meat, chopped into small pieces
800g - 1lb 12oz rice
1 onion finely chopped
4 packets fresh dill, chopped finely
olive or sunflower oil
1 small packet frozen broad beans
2 potatoes, peeled and cut into 5mm - ¼ inch slices
3 glasses water
2.5ml - ½tsp turmeric
2.5ml - ½tsp black pepper
2.5ml - ½tsp salt
5ml - 1tsp powdered saffron
⅓ glass boiling water

Method

Wash and soak the rice for 1 hour. Wash the meat and mix with salt, pepper and turmeric.
Fry the onion in a little oil until golden brown. Add the meat, stir for a few minutes and then add the water.
Cover with lid and cook for almost 45 minutes or until tender.
Meanwhile, boil some water and skin the beans. Cook them in the salted water until almost tender.
In a large pan, cook the rice with 25ml - 5 tsp salt. Just before the rice is cooked add the dill and the peeled half cooked beans to the boiling water. Mix very well.
Drain in a colander, pouring cold water to refresh the rice. Drain well.
Take out 2 cups of rice and set aside. In the same pan-which has been washed and dried - heat about 20ml - 4tsp oil.
Take the pan off the heat and, in layers, place the potato slices on the base, half the rice, the meat and then the other half of the rice. Over this pour in one glass of the stock left from the meat pan.
Then take the 2 cups of rice which were set aside and mix in the saffron water until the rice takes up the wonderful colour.
Add this to the pan and shape into a mould, not flat as for biryani.
Wrap the lid of the pan in a clean teacloth and replace firmly on the pan. Cook on lowest flame for almost 45 minutes until the steam has escaped.
Serve in a large platter, decorating with the golden rice from the top.
This absolutely delicious and attractive meal is now ready to serve.
Vegetarians can use soya or quorn instead of meat.

Stuffed Green Chillies

Stuffed chillies are usually eaten with a rice dish. The stuffing can vary enormously. The inhabitants of the tropics recognise it as an appetite stimulator, although nowadays the younger generation don't seem to be too adventurous. Many households still recognise them. Not as hot as you would think but certainly a good crunch and a enhancer for many bland meals including yoghurt. Because the seeds are removed it isn't as hot as one may think.

Ingredients

12 green jalepeno chillies
2.5ml - ½tsp turmeric
2.5ml - ½tsp ground mustard
1.25ml - ¼tsp salt
1.25ml - ¼tsp cumin powder
1.25ml - ¼tsp garam masala
15ml - 1tbsp gram flour
15ml - 1tbsp yoghurt
vegetable oil for shallow frying

Method

Wash the chillies and slit cutting halfway through, carefully take out the membrane and seeds and wash with cold water.
Combine the ingredients and enough yoghurt to make a paste and evenly fill the cavities of the chilli.
Heat the oil in a fry pan and on the lowest heat fry the chillies until slightly crispy carefully turning over just once and fry until slightly blistered.
Remove with a slotted spoon and drain on a kitchen towel.
Serve hot or cold.

Poppy Seed Potatoes

These steamed potatoes are marinated in seasoned yoghurt before browning therefore the aromatic flavour seems to permeate every bite.
You could eat this with a leavened bread or even with a green salad when entertaining.

Ingredients

55g - 2oz white poppy seeds, soaked overnight and washed and drained
2 green chillies
60ml - 4tbsp chopped fresh coconut
180ml - 6 fl oz yoghurt
10 medium sized new potatoes, steamed and cut into 1" cubes
60ml - 4tbsp ghee or vegetable oil
5ml - 1 tsp cumin seeds
2.5ml - ½tsp onion seeds
1 bayleaf
2.5ml - ½tsp turmeric
5ml - 1tsp salt
30ml - 2tbsp lime juice

Method

Combine the poppy seeds with the chillies, fresh coriander, coconut and yoghurt.
Process until well blended.
Mix the seasoned yoghurt well with the potatoes and cover and leave in the fridge for 3 hours.
Heat the oil or ghee in a non stick frying pan and when hot, but not smoking. Add the cumin seeds, onion seeds and bayleaf and when they have stopped spluttering add the potatoes, turmeric and salt and mix well stirring all the time.
Reduce the heat and cook until the potatoes are dry and the outside is crusty and golden.
Sprinkle with lime juice just before serving.

Top Left: Mixed Vegetables & Turnip Front Right: Mattar Paneer

King Prawn Biryani

Biryani

Biryani, among all the exotic recipes in Asian cuisine, is the most royal of dishes. It is served on religious and other auspicious occasions as well as at large family gatherings. Whether biryani is served to welcome guests on the first day of their visit, or whether it is the main course for a formal gathering or a festival, the care taken in its preparation begins with the selection of ingredients. Nothing but the best will do.

Basmati rice - known as the 'queen of rice'- is a vital ingredient. Finely sliced onions are fried until golden, meat is marinated in curds and saffron is used to add a unique flavour and aroma to the dish. Saffron is also used as a colouring agent and a tenderiser. Indeed, there is no other ingredient like it.

Biryani is a rice dish cooked with either meat, fish or mince. The various ingredients are cooked in one pot but ingeniously kept in separate layers.

Chicken Biryani

Ingredients

1 large chicken, chopped in pieces and washed
2 large onions, finely sliced
3 large potatoes, peeled and cut in bite-size pieces
4 hard boiled eggs

For the marinade

8 green chillies - pounded fine
45ml - 3tbsp yoghurt
30ml - 2tbsp ginger paste
15ml - 1tbsp garlic paste
30ml - 2tbsp turmeric
75ml - 5tbsp coriander powder
salt to taste
2.5ml - ½tbsp garam masala
425g - 15oz tin of chopped tomatoes
some cardammon, cinnamon and cumin seeds
175g - 6oz frozen green peas (boiled masoor may be used instead)
a few strands saffron steeped in boiled milk, ghee and oil
600g - 1lb 5oz basmati rice

Method

Make a marinade with the ingredients listed. Marinate chicken pieces overnight or for a few hours, stirring occasionally.

In a large saucepan melt 30ml - 2tbsp ghee with 30ml - 2tbsp vegetable oil. Add onions and fry on low heat until golden brown and crisp. Take care not to burn the onions. Take out the fried onions using a slotted spoon. Place the marinated chicken in the pan, cover and cook on medium heat.

Meanwhile, fry the potatoes coloured with turmeric and seasoned with salt- in oil until cooked and golden. Boil and shell the eggs.

Turn the meat occasionally. Switch off the heat when the meat has cooked and the moisture has evaporated.

Put 30ml - 2tbsp of ghee in a frying pan. Cook the tomatoes, spices and peas until almost dry.

Steep the saffron in a few tablespoons of hot milk. Boil some water in a large pot with 15ml - 3 tsp salt.

Wash and drain the rice and add to the boiling water. Boil on medium heat until almost cooked, taking care not to over-cook.

Drain rice in a colander and run cold water over it to remove excess starch and refresh the rice. In the same large pot put 30ml - 2tbsp ghee and 30ml - 2tbsp cooking oil.

Then start to make the layers. First sprinkle a handful of rice to cover the base, arrange potatoes, sprinkle some of the fried onions and make a layer with the rice. Then make a layer of the meat, tomatoes and peas mix. Add more fried onions and rice.

Carry on in this fashion, distributing evenly and using up all the prepared food. Save a few onions for the top of the last layer of rice.

Pour in the saffron and milk mix, together with half a 125ml - 4 fl oz water, around the pot. Cover with foil and place the lid on top, allowing no steam to escape.

Place over high heat for five minutes and then simmer for one hour. After this time all the moisture should have evaporated and the rice will have finished cooking.

The different shades of colour will be apparent on serving- white rice, yellow rice, green peas, golden onions and finally the chopped green coriander.

Cut the eggs lengthways and decorate the biryani - a dish fit for royalty.

Fish Biryani

Biryani is a dish for special occasions. Whether to welcome guests or when entertaining, the time and care taken in making biryani is certainly worthwhile.
This attention to detail begins with the selection of ingredients - nothing but the best will do.
The pride and care that goes into making biryani is a story in itself, from the weighing of the saffron and frying of the onions to a particular shade of gold, to the sealing of the pot with a clean white cloth, and weighing down of the lid with a heavy load, least steam should escape.
It is important to listen carefully to ascertain whether it is the moisture or ghee that is sizzling.
Fish biryani has a unique flavour. Any variety of firm white fish can be used. I prefer fish steaks from a large cod with any bones removed so you can eat the meal without having to worry about the bones, especially as it is also intended for young children.
Yoghurt, salt, cumin powder and green chillies blended together is the perfect accompaniment.
Fish biryani would make a delicious change from the usual festive feast of turkey and is a delight for those occasions when families get together.

Ingredients

900g - 2lb fish steaks (cod or coley)
115g - 4oz masoor (black lentils)
3 medium onions, very finely sliced
45ml - 3tbsp tomato puree
250ml - 9 fl oz yoghurt
800g - 1lb 12oz rice & 20ml - 4tsp salt boiled together
4 green chillies (adjust to taste)
2.5ml - ½tsp turmeric
2.5ml - ½tsp cumin seeds
4 pods cardammon
a few sticks cinnamon
a few whole peppercorns
3 medium potatoes, peeled, cut into pieces and deep fried in oil
4 hard boiled eggs
ghee & oil
5ml - 1tsp saffron
fresh coriander leaves- washed and finely chopped

Fish Masala

30ml - 2tbsp coriander powder
7 cloves garlic
6 green chillies
15ml - 1tbsp cumin powder
juice of 1 fresh lemon
5ml - 1tsp turmeric
15ml - 1tbsp oil
salt to taste

Method

Wash the boneless fish steaks. With a very sharp knife cut into chunks and drain.
Pound together the garlic, coriander powder, chillies and cumin. Add the other dry spices and mix into a paste with the lemon juice and oil. Smear the fish slices with this masala. Marinate for an hour.
Meanwhile, boil the washed rice until almost done. Drain and refresh with cold water to remove excess starch.
Wash and boil the lentils until almost tender. In a few tablespoons of oil fry the onions on low heat until golden and crisp. Remove with a slotted spoon. In the same pan (adding more oil if necessary) fry the fish a few pieces at a time until it is just firm. Remove from the oil.
Mix together the yoghurt, tomato puree, spices and half the finely sliced onions. Pour over the fried fish.
Into a heavy-based pot, pour some oil and 45ml - 3tbsp ghee. Turn on the heat to the lowest setting. Sprinkle half the lentils over the base. Carefully arrange the fish and excess masala over the lentils.
Add the rest of the lentils and arrange the fried potatoes to which a sprinkling of salt and turmeric has been added.
Next, layer the rice but keep about one and a half cups.
Lastly, add the fried onions and pour the saffron water (125ml - 4 fl oz hot water and few strands pounded saffron) into the rest of the rice. Mix well to give the rice a rich golden colour. Add this as the last layer.
Turn on the heat until the pot starts sizzling, then put the heat to its lowest, making sure no steam escapes from the tight-fitting lid.
Allow steaming for about 30-45 minutes.
When serving, decorate with eggs and chopped coriander.
Lift out the fish slices carefully.
Serve with chutney, papadums, spiced yoghurt or pickles.

King Prawn Palau

Madras is a land of surf, spice and magic. The shade of the banyan tree, heady in scent and spices.
Of the coast of the Tamil Nadu, out in the Bengal Bay, lie the Nicobar Islands where the crystal clear waters shimmer with tropical fish among the coral. Though Tamilians have their own history and traditions, something all Indians have in common is hospitality teamed with excellent food and gracious service. Food is traditionally served on platters with raised edges, called thal for men and thali for women. to eat, most families sit on woven mats. Richer Tamilians sit on sheets that are richly coloured and painted with hand blocks, large and exceptionally tasty prawns are caught in the waters around Madras, the combination of delicious juicy prawns and fragrance of spices make a remarkable palau dish. Tiger prawns are recommended but, if frozen prawns are used thaw and clean well before cooking.

Ingredients

1 small onion chopped finely
600g - 1lb 5oz basmati rice
30ml - 2tbsp oil
30ml - 2tbsp ghee
2.5ml - ½tsp cumin seeds
10ml - 2tsp ginger/garlic paste
10ml - 2tsp chilli powder
2.5ml - ½tsp turmeric
salt to taste
450g - 1lb king prawns
30ml - 2tbsp yoghurt
4 green chillies
10ml - 2tsp lemon juice
3 green cardammon pods
4 bayleaves
few cloves
2 sticks cinammon
1 spring onion, chopped
55g - 2oz green peas
fresh coriander, chopped

Method

Wash rice and soak for 20 mins. Drain well and heat oil/ghee in a medium sized heavy pan. Add cumin seeds and onion and let them sizzle. Add ginger/garlic paste, chilli powder, turmeric and salt. Stir for a while add prawns, then add the yoghurt. Cook briefly over a medium heat. Add the green chillies and let the moisture evaporate. Cook the peas or lentils adding remaining chillies and salt stir in the lemon juice adding the other spices, to the water.
Bring to the boil and add the drained rice for a few minutes until partially cooked.
Combine the peas or lentils with the rice and mix in the fresh coriander leaves gently with a fork (leaving some for the garnish).
Make layers in a clean pan, first the rice, then the prawn mixture and spring onions, finishing of with a layer of rice.
Sprinkle a few spoons of hot water over the top cover tightly and cook on the lowest heat for a further 30 minutes.
Garnish with the remaining fresh green coriander just before serving.

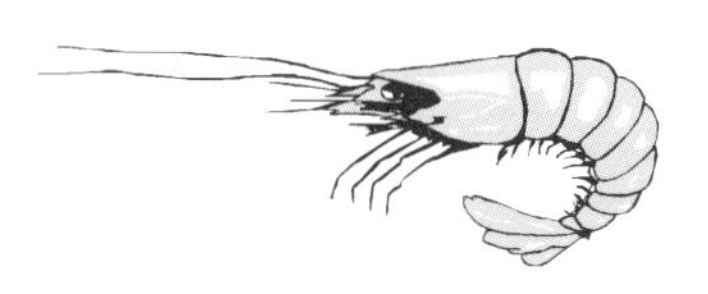

Vegetable Biryani

Ingredients

500g - llb 2oz basmati rice
60ml - 4tbsp ghee
5 cardammon pods
5 cloves
5 peppercorns
5 bay leaves
10ml - 2tsp cumin seeds
few sticks cinammon
5ml - 1tsp turmeric
12.5ml - 2½tsp salt
2 medium onions chopped
60g - 2oz golden raisins
115g - 4oz frozen peas
115g - 4oz mixed frozen vegetables
crispy golden fried onions and slivered green chillies for garnish
1200ml - 2pt boiling water

Method

In a sieve, rinse the rice until the water runs clear, drain well.
Heat the ghee in a pan and fry the spices and onion until golden brown taking care not to over brown. Stir in the washed rice mixing well then add the stock and boiling water. Cover well
and reduce heat and cook gently for about 15 minutes.
Add the peas and frozen vegetables and raisins return to the heat for a further 15 minutes.
Serve hot, fluffing up with a fork and decorate with onion rings and flaked almonds.

Zarda

Zarda, or sometimes pronounced as jarda is a sweet saffron rice dish. Sweet, colourful and decorated with exotic ingredients such as pistachio nuts, almonds, coconuts,cardommon and the liberal use of saffron.
Zarda is usually associated with biryani. Present on the table at auspicious celebrations and gatherings. Rice has been the staple diet of Asians since ancient times. India, China and java each lay claim to have been the first to cultivate the crop on their land. Many beautiful myths have been woven around the theme of the rice. In Indian scripts rice was mentioned as early as 2,800BC, although the grain is known throughout the world with various names.
Zarda is a very attractive dish with the bright orange colouring, the glossiness from the syrup and the colourful decorations of the nuts and raisin, glazed cherries of assorted colours available today and the pineapple and not to forget the freshly grated coconut.
A delicious variety almost to good to eat after all a dish made wholeheartedly with care and precision should not only be tasty to the palette but also pleasing to the eye.

Ingredients

400g - 14oz basmati or any other rice
75ml - 5tbsp melted ghee
5ml - 1tsp saffron
3 cinammon sticks
few green cardommon pods
glace cherries of different colours, chopped small
60ml - 4tbsp freshly grated coconut
5ml - 1tsp cardammon powder
slivered almonds
a generous handful of slivered pistachio nuts
orange colouring powder
and some chunks of tinned pineapple pieces

Syrup

400g - 14oz sugar
300ml - 10 fl oz water
few strands saffron
orange colouring

Method

Boil the washed rice with a pinch of colour until well cooked but not over soft. Run cold water over the rice rinsing the starch and drain in a colander. Leave to drain meanwhile prepare the syrup.
In a saucepan melt the ghee add the cinammon, cardammon, sultanas,and braise till shiny then add the sugar and water and saffron.
Boil rapidly till a syrup of medium consistency is achieved. Taking care not to make it too thick or it will crystallise.
Now add the syrup to the rice and mix well in a large pot incorporating all the ingredients together and making sure the syrup has covered the rice. Add a few spoons of syrup from the pineapple tin and the remaining ingredients.
At this stage it is a good idea to let it all settle and allow the rice to fully absorb the syrup for a couple of hours if time permits.
Alternatively if cooking straightaway allow to cook very slowly under low heat until all moisture evaporates.
Serve hot on attractive platters decorated with nuts and coconut.

Sweet Saffron Rice

An alternative to the regular Zarda

Ingredients

105ml - 7tbsp ghee
4 cardammon pods
2 small pieces cinammon stick
280g - 10oz basmati rice
600ml - 1pt hot water
5ml - 1tsp saffron strands
280g - 10oz caster sugar
10ml - 2tsp warm milk
10ml - 2tsp raisins
30ml - 2tbsp flaked almonds
10ml - 2tsp ground pistachio
2.5ml - ½tsp cardammon powder
2.5ml - ½tsp nutmeg powder

Method

Heat half the ghee in pan and fry the cardammon pods and the cinammon sticks. Add the washed and drained rice and fry until shiny, pour in the hot water and bring to the boil. Reduce the heat and cover partially cook until the rice is fluffy and simmer until dry. Meanwhile mix the saffron into the milk and gently fold into the rice, along with all the other ingredients. Blend well with a fork and simmer again on the lowest heat. Serve warm dribbled with melted ghee.

Plain Saffron Rice

This golden rice is easy to make and extremely delicious with the hint of the saffron. It can be eaten with almost any sort of curry but when serving kebab or karai meat, fried fish on this bed of rice, the contrast of colours looks so appealing it is almost too good to eat.

Ingredients

450g - 1lb basmati rice
700ml - 1¼pt water
3 green cardammon pods
2 cloves
5ml - 1tsp salt
2.5ml - ½tsp crushed saffron strands
45ml - 3tbsp milk

Method

Rinse the rice in a sieve until all the water runs clear.
In a non stick pan pour the water and add the rice, throw in all the whole spices and the salt and bring to the boil. Cover and simmer for almost 10 minutes. Meanwhile in a small cup pour the milk and saffron and microwave for a minute or boil in a small pan. Cook the rice until it is soft on the outside but just slightly hard on the inside.
Carefully drain the rice in a colander and drain.
Replace in the pan and pour the saffron milk over the top of the rice.
Cover with a tight fitting lid and place the pan back on the lowest heat until steam escapes and the rice is thoroughly cooked.

Pilau Rice

Rice is a cereal crop which is eaten as a staple food in many parts of the world.
Like potatoes, it is only a slimmer's friend if fat or oil is not used in the cooking or serving.
The rice available in shops can be divided into two basic groups- short grain that is used in desserts and long grain that is used for savoury dishes.
Long grain white rice has its husk, germ and most of its bran layers removed by a 'polishing' process.
This variety, with its long and slender grain, originates from the Patna region of India but it is also grown in the United States and Thailand.
Long grain rice usually accompanies curries, casseroles or stews. It is also used for salads or added to dishes such as kedgeree or paella.
Only the inedible husk is removed from brown rice, leaving a light brown grain. The bran layer, providing fibre beneficial amounts of vitamin B, minerals and proteins, is kept.
The minerals are concentrated in the skins of the rice and are lost if the grain is polished.
Brown rice has a slightly nutty flavour and crunchier texture than white rice. Many people consider it to be tastier. However, it does take longer to cook.
Nature has blessed Basmati rice with the quality of reaching the peak of perfection with little external help. This places Basmati in a class of its own.
Basmati costs a little more but the end result makes it worth every additional penny.
Not only is it easier to cook, its unique taste, flavour and aroma add a special quality to a meal.
The distinct flavour of Basmati rice is an integral part of the taste of such authentic Oriental dishes as pilaus, pilafs and biryanis.
Italian rice has a large, round grain with a texture ideal for risotto.
Short grain rice-also know as pudding rice or short round grain rice- is rounded and plump with a chalky colour. This variety, when cooked, is more moist than long grain rice and tends to stick.
Short grain rice-made by grinding long grain rice- is used in puddings and in baking.

Ingredients

400g - 14oz basmati white rice
10ml - 2tsp salt
30ml - 2tbsp ghee
15ml - 1tbsp vegetable oil
½ small, finely sliced onion
a few pieces cinnamon
cardammon pods
2.5ml - ½tsp cumin seeds
1.3 ltr - 2¼pt boiling water

Method

Fry onions in ghee until slightly golden. Add cumin seeds and spices. Quickly add water, salt and the washed and drained rice.
Boil on medium heat until the water is absorbed.
Then reduce the heat to a minimum until all moisture has evaporated and the rice is fluffy.
The oil or ghee should be omitted for diabetics or those who need to be conscious about their weight. In this case, boil the rice until three-quarter cooked. Rinse the rice under running hot water to remove starch and simmer on low heat until cooked.

Spicy Rice

Ingredients

115g - 4oz ghee
2 medium onions chopped
5ml - 1tsp saffron strands
500g - 1lb 2oz rice
10ml - 2tsp cumin seeds
10ml - 2tsp salt
115g - 4oz flaked toasted almonds

Method

Heat the ghee in a heavy pan and fry the onion until golden.
Add the saffron strands and cumin seeds and fry for a further minute.
Add the rice and fry for 5 minutes until the moisture has been absorbed and the colour has escaped from the saffron onto the rice tinting it beautifully.
Add salt and enough water about 4 cups and simmer until the rice is tender and cooked and all the moisture has evaporated serve with toasted almonds and meted warm ghee sprinkled over the top.

Aromatic Rice

Ingredients

15ml - 1tbsp oil
15ml - 1tbsp ghee
5 bay leaves
2 cinammon sticks
8 green cardammons
500g - 1lb 2oz basmati rice
10ml - 2tsp salt

Method

Heat the oil/ghee in a heavy based pan. Fry the spices and bay leaves for a few seconds until a wonderful aroma imparts. Add the washed and drained rice and enough boiling water to cover the rice, about 4 cups.
Cover with a tight fitting lid and simmer for about 30 minutes, until all the water has been absorbed, and the rice is cooked and fluffy ready to serve.

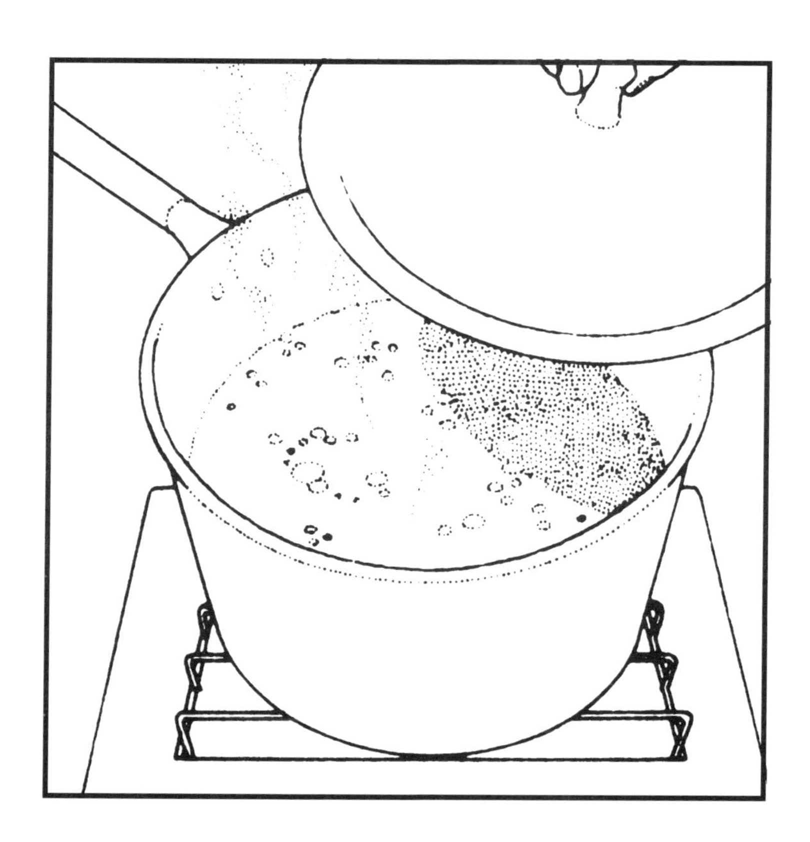

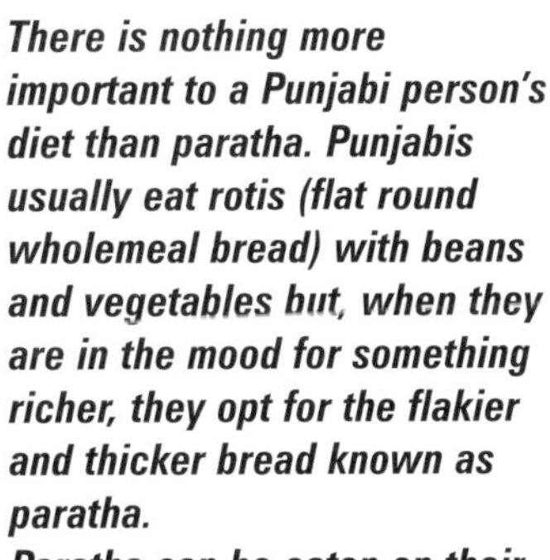

Paratha

There is nothing more important to a Punjabi person's diet than paratha. Punjabis usually eat rotis (flat round wholemeal bread) with beans and vegetables but, when they are in the mood for something richer, they opt for the flakier and thicker bread known as paratha.

Paratha can be eaten on their own, with curries or with a range of fillings. And potatoes or spinach can be eaten with a bowl of yoghurt in which the paratha is dipped.

Rice may do for special occasions or for making rice pudding but the only food that makes a true Punjabi feel he has eaten a proper, filling meal is paratha.

This recipe is for deep-fried paratha, which is simple to make and takes very little time.

Paratha is best eaten with rich curries. It teams up perfectly with rogan josh, which would be the ideal dish to serve for the Muslim festival of Eid-Ul-Adha when meat is cooked and eaten in abundance.

Ingredients

275g - 9½ oz plain flour
20ml - 4tsp baking powder
30ml - 2tbsp melted ghee
2.5ml - ½tsp salt
20ml - 4tsp sugar
125ml - 4 fl oz cold water
125ml - 4 fl oz cold milk
1 egg
sesame seeds
oil for deep-frying

Method

Sift the plain flour and baking powder. Rub in the ghee until it resembles fine breadcrumbs.
Add sugar and salt and bind in the beaten egg, leaving aside a little to glaze 10 discs. Make a firm, pliable dough with the milk and water mixed together.
Using only as much as you need, divide into 10 balls. Roll each one out into circles about 5mm - ¼ inch thick.
When the discs have all been rolled out brush with beaten egg and sprinkle with sesame seeds.
Heat the oil until very hot. Fry one at a time, making sure the side with the seeds is at the top.
The paratha will start puffing up almost immediately. Turn over on to the other side and drain well.
Fry all the paratha individually. Serve hot or store in an airtight container.

Kani Roti

Ingredients

115g - 4oz rice flour - sieved
5ml - 1tsp salt
cold water
vegetable oil for smearing

Method

With the cold water make a batter almost the consistency of pancake mixture but slightly thinner.
Heat a skillet or a non stick frying pan and drop ½ spoon of oil in and swivel around so not a spot is left ungreased. Pour enough batter and cover the entire area into an even circle and when the edges start peeling carefully lift the circle and turn over taking care not to brown. The colour should be as white as possible.
Turn over once more and lift out almost immediately. Once the skill is acquired you will be churning these out in no time.
Usually eaten with a thin chicken soup.

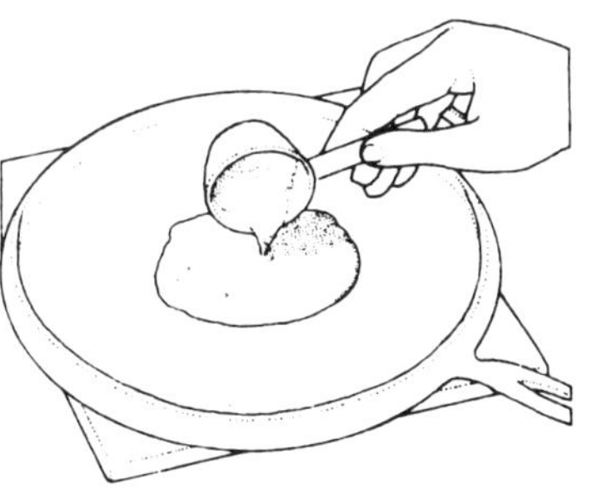

Kashmiri Puree

The addition of the aniseed makes this puree unique it has a taste which is extremely unusual yet delectable, and easily recognised to come from Kashmir

Ingredients

125ml - 4 fl oz warm milk
140g - 5oz fine whole wheat flour
140g - 5oz plain white flour
10ml - 2tsp sugar
15ml - 1tbsp aniseed roasted on a griddle and ground into fine powder
5ml - 1tsp dried yeast
10 strands saffron soaked in warm milk
a good pinch of salt
30ml - 2tbsp yoghurt
5ml - 1tsp poppy seeds
oil for frying

Method

Sprinkle the teaspoon of sugar and yeast over the warm milk until frothy.
Sieve together the flours and salt add the remaining sugar and aniseed powder.
Gradually pour in the yeast mixture and make a soft dough, adding extra milk if necessary.
Knead well and cover with a damp cloth. Leave for 4-6 hours in a warm place.
Knead well again and divide into 16 portions.
On a lightly floured board roll out into 4" circles.
Mix the saffron milk, yoghurt and poppy seeds together and leave for 1 minute.
Heat the oil in a deep pan and smear the puri with the saffron milk on both sides and lower gently into the oil until it puffs up.
Turn over and remove when golden brown. It is best to fry only two purees at a time.

Wheatflour - Everyday Roti

Rotis are a type of unleavened bread. Although many varieties can be made this is the one that is traditionally made every day in the average Indian household.

Ingredients

2.5ml - ½tsp salt
55g - 2oz butter or ghee
350g - 12oz chappatti flour
175g - 6oz or more of boiled water
30ml - 2tbsp ghee for frying

Method

Rub the salt and fat into the flour until you have a breadcrumb consistency.
Gradually add the water until a soft and pliable dough is formed making sure it is not too soft.
Divide the dough into 8 balls and knead each one individually until it is smooth and round.
Roll out onto a floured board into a neat circle. Heat a chappatti pan or griddle and cook the roti on both sides allowing it to puff up.
Dribble the melted ghee over the top and remove from the heat now fry the next one.
Carry on until all the rotis are cooked and piled up ready to be eaten.

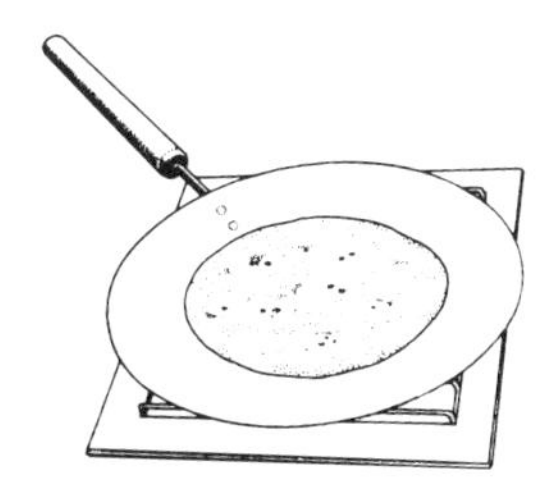

Jeera Puree

These purees are delicious flavoured with cumin and sesame seeds and puff up really well. They can be eaten with afternoon tea or even with chutneys for a small snack.

Ingredients

115g - 4oz whole wheat flour
2.5ml - ½tsp salt
2.5ml - ½tsp cumin seeds
2.5ml - ½tsp freshly ground pepper
7.5ml - 1½tsp sesame seeds
25g - 1oz melted butter
warm water to make a firm dough
oil for deep frying

Method

Mix together all the dry ingredients in a bowl, add the butter and rub to resemble bread crumbs. Slowly add just enough water and knead into a firm dough, cover with a damp cloth and leave to rest for 15 minutes.
Make 16 balls and roll into a circle about 3" diameter lightly prick each puree several times with a fork and heat oil in a karai and fry until they puff only 3 at a time for about 30 seconds on each side.They should be a lovely golden brown drain on absorbent paper.

Dahi Puree

Dahi puree are deep fried puree enriched with yoghurt and butter. Best eaten immediately for the fuller flavour.

Ingredients

450g - 16oz whole wheat flour
2.5ml - ½tsp bicarbonate of soda
5ml - 1tsp baking powder
250ml - 9 fl oz yoghurt
25g - 1oz butter
oil for deep frying

Method

Mix the flour, soda and baking powder into a bowl.
Rub in the butter and slowly add the yoghurt until a soft dough is formed. Knead for 10 minutes.
Put the dough in a clean polythene bag and tie a knot.
Leave for 8 hours to rest.
Take out and knead again.
Divide the dough into 30 balls, cover tightly again for 15 minutes.
Roll each ball to a small circle and fry in deep oil. They should puff up immediately.
A tasty variation would be to add fresh coriander or fenugreek leaves for flavour.

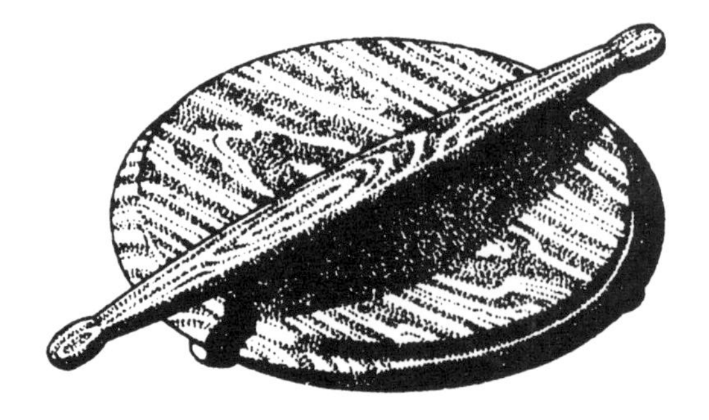

Roti & Puree

Deep Fried Tilapia Fillet & Saffron Rice

Chambo Fish

Malawi has to be the opening country to the International section as this country is always special to me being the country where I was born. Malawi is often referred to as the warm heart of Africa, and not without reason too. It has the greatest assets any land can have - contrast. The contrast between lowland and mountain plateau, between the lake as large as an inland sea and tropical waters, between forests, grassland and dams. What is remarkable about the country is that in the field of conservation she started of with virtually nothing at the time of her Independence, yet today her five national parks provide a conservation backbone and the government have a reputation to ensure their protection. On a continent known for its vast expanses of often desolute country. Malawi is refreshingly a compact area of diverse beauty. Mountains carpeted with unique wild flowers and forests of towering cedar trees. A host of lakes and rivers and Lake Malawi being the third largest lake in Africa is often referred to as Livingstone's 'lake of stars.'
It is in this crystal clear lake that many species of fish are found.
The fresh vegetation and crops the tea estates all have a special part to play in the economy of the country. The freshness is remarkable and all to often there will be the locals arriving early in the mornings to sell their produce, be it fresh vegetables, eggs or fruit. But it is at the lake that the best fish is sold, freshly caught and still flapping in the net. Mention chambo and immediately Malawi springs to mind. The chambo fish is very popular there and is avaialble here too.

Ingredients

5ml - 1tsp salt
2.5ml - ½tsp cumin powder
2.5ml - ½tsp coriander powder
3 fresh green chillies
55g - 2oz fresh chopped coriander
10ml - 2tsp garlic paste
fresh karipulya leaves
5 medium onions
2 chambo or tilapia fish cut into 1" thick slices
juice of 2 lemons
½ bunch shallots
8 large tomatoes
3 green peppers
1 red pepper
75ml - 5tbsp tomato puree
10ml - 2tsp chilli powder
5ml - 1tsp tabasco sauce
oil for frying

Method

Heat the oil and fry the onions till soft and lightly golden.
While they are frying make a marinade using the first 7 ingredients.
Marinate the washed fish and leave for a while. It can be marinated for a few hours if time permits allowing the fish to have a fuller flavour.
Add the remaining ingredients with the fried onions and cook over a low heat until all moisture has evaporated.
Sprinkle the fish with a little flour to prevent sticking to the pan and fry in deep oil turning over until cooked.
Lift out with a slotted spoon and serve with the sauce over the top.

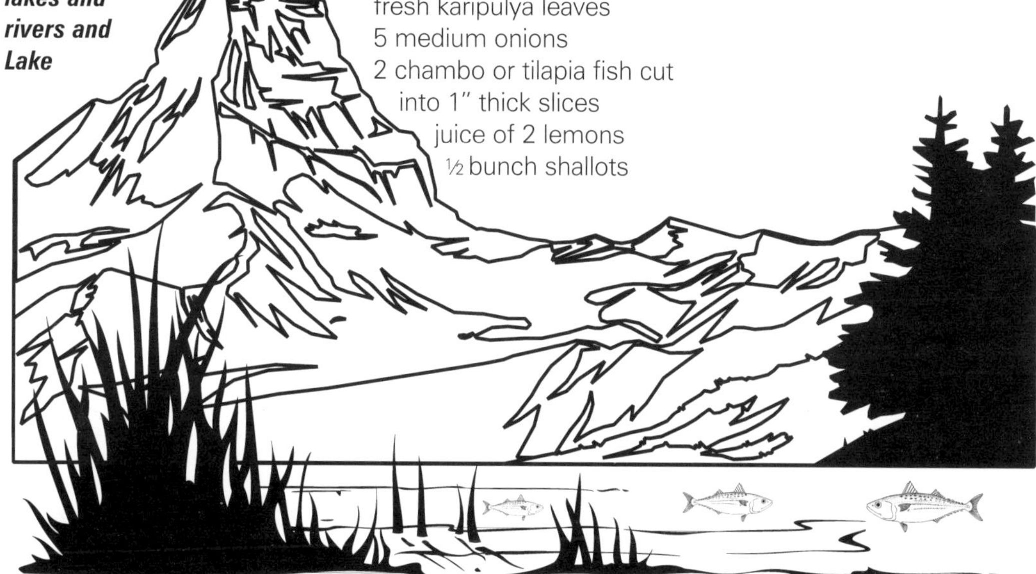

Mishshi

Arabian cooking techniques are economical and uncomplicated because they evolved from a nomadic life in which simplicity was most important.
Although diverse influences from North Africa, Spain, Portugal, and other neighbouring countries produced a multi-faceted and rich cuisine of beautiful and elaborate dishes, the original Bedouin style has stood the test of time.
The economy and simplicity of this form of Arabian cuisine is enhanced by the imaginative use of seasoning, colour and presentation.
Hospitality to visitors, friends or strangers is a serious obligation and duty as well as a pleasure.
Food and drink are automatically offered to guests and they should not be refused. A meal is served either on a cloth spread over a carpet on a large brass or copper tray resting on legs. Guests sit on low cushions around the food. All the dishes are presented simultaneously and eaten in order of preference.
Where possible the Arabian cook uses unrefined ingredients for dishes prepared for a combination of meat, fish, poultry, grain, pulses and vegetables.
A generous use of herbs and spices is common in Arabic cookery. Mezze appetisers are part of the Arabic way of life. The more auspicious the occasion the wider the variety of mezze offered.
These appetisers are prepared in numerous ways. The selection offered is limited only by the cook's repertoire and the ingredients available.
Dolmas or the Arabic 'mishshi' is a general name for stuffed vegetables. As far as mezze are concerned the name usually refers to stuffed vine or cabbage leaves.
Canned vine leaves- available from most supermarkets- are a delicious alternative to cabbage and easier to handle.
The stuffing is either rice and mince ground lamb or rice and vegetables.
If the dolmas or mishshi are to be served hot then they should be accompanied by a bowl of yoghurt.

Ingredients

200g - 7oz basmati rice
1 medium onion, chopped finely
10ml - 2tsp tomato paste
10ml - 2tsp garlic paste
10ml - 2tsp green chilli paste
5ml - 1tsp mint sauce
salt & pepper to taste
1 medium potato, peeled and chopped small
1 cabbage
1 fresh lemon
30ml - 2tbsp olive oil

Method

Cook the washed rice with 7.5ml 1½ tsp salt and the chopped potato.
When just cooked drain in a colander and wash out the starch by pouring cold water over.
Drain the mixture. Add the tomato and garlic, chillies, mint, salt and pepper. Mix well, and leave to cool.
Meanwhile, wash the cabbage and trim off the stalk. Strip off the leaves carefully and cut out any hard central stalks.
Wash them again and dip them, a few at a time, into a pan of boiling salted water until they become wilted.
If this is difficult to do then put the whole cabbage in the pan of boiling water for about five minutes.
Lift out the cabbage, drain and peel off the leaves. Place 15ml - 1tsbp of the rice mixture on to the leaves and roll tightly, folding in the sides as you go.
Layer the stuffed leaves, seasoned side down, in a pan lined with torn leaves.
When complete, sprinkle with the lemon juice and oil and add enough water to just cover the leaves.
Place a heavy plate over the top, replace the lid of the pan and simmer gently for one hour. Drain and eat either hot or cold.

While the word pasta conjures up images of the warmth and hospitality of Italian people, it is not the only food eaten by Italians, as some would have us believe.
However, pasta does represent a very important part of the Italian daily diet. Each Italian consumes the equivalent of 35kg pasta each year but the equivalent in Britain is only 1.5kg per person.
The use of pasta is increasing every year by approximately 20%.
The history of pasta in Italy has been the subject of great debate. Records show that the ancient Romans ate pasta as early as the 4th or 5th century.
The exact nutritional value of pasta varies but good quality brands contain as much as 13% protein as well as vitamins, minerals and a small amount of fat.
Pasta is high in carbohydrate. Usually, the sauce with it is more fattening than the pasta itself. The finest commercial pasta is made from durum wheat that is mostly imported from Canada. Dried pasta, like spaghetti and other tubular varieties, is more common in southern Italy and abroad than in the north of Italy where pasta is more likely to be of the flat kind often made with fresh eggs.
Pasta with eggs has more protein and extra bite. It is popular among athletes as it sustains energy levels.
Interest in diet suggests we have a lot to learn from the Mediterranean style of cooking. In the south of Italy, where olive oil is used most for cooking and where pasta, vegetables and fruit are eaten in abundance, there is little consumption of meat and animal products.
This type produces a lower incidence of coronary heart disease and related conditions.
The Italians have invented more than 300 different shapes of pasta. You might think they wanted to confuse us with all the different names!
However, each variety is suited to a particular sauce or dish. So, don't be put off by the choice- the variety makes so much fun.
The shape is more important than you might think. Serious pleasure can be gained from eating the right combination of texture, shape and flavour.
The Italian pasta company Voiello commissioned car designer Giugiaro to come up with a technically perfect shape of pasta, not for its aerodynamics, but so that it would collect as much sauce as possible to make each morsel succulent and delicious.
The designer's peculiar construction was a short tube, ridged inside and with wings. This pasta is called marille.
Different colours are available- green is usually coloured with spinach and red with beetroot. This gives pasta an individual taste and enhances the appearance of any dish.
This recipe is a mixture of Italian and Asian cuisine. Asian ingredients give pasta a taste of its own. It is a favourite among all ages.
The following recipe is a combination of two pastas - conchiglie, a shell shaped pasta, and green tortiglioni, a spiral shaped pasta.
Chicken has been included here but soya meat can be used instead for vegetarians.

Ingredients

2 chicken breasts, washed and diced
1 cup conchiglie
1 cup tortiglioni
425g - 15oz tin chopped tomatoes
1 small onion, finely sliced
1 red, 1 green and 1 yellow pepper, washed, de-seeded and cubed
½ cup frozen sweetcorn
½ cup baby sweetcorn
45ml - 3tbsp olive oil
a hint of turmeric
3 chopped green chillies
30ml - 2tbsp garlic paste
salt & pepper to taste
175g - 6oz cheese for topping

Method

Boil the pasta according to the instructions on the packet. Refresh with cold water and drain.
Warm the olive oil in a saucepan and add the onions until softened.
To this add the chicken and spices. Cook on medium heat until the moisture has evaporated.
Add the tomatoes and stir until almost dry. Mix in the remaining ingredients except the cheese.
When the sauce is thicker and almost dry transfer to a casserole, top with the cheese. Cook in a hot oven for 15 minutes until the cheese has melted and is golden brown.
The dish is now ready to serve.

Couscous

Couscous is a North African dish.
The name applies both to the grains which resembles semolina and and also to the whole dish.
It is thought that the word originated from the French sutsoo which describes the sound the vapour makes when it passes through the grain as it steams.
Couscous is served in large round shallow dishes and the grains are heaped up like a mountain with a shallow depression on the top. The chunks of meat are placed in the well and vegetable at the sides. Almost all the couscous here is commercially pre cooked which only needs a little water adding and heating through.
With care the couscous can be perfectly cooked.
This is a recipe I picked up from my vacation in Tunisia, where a local family insisted on inviting us for a traditional Tunisian meal.

Ingredients

450g - 1lb meat
3 small onions quartered and thickly sliced
pinch of saffron threads
10ml - 2tsp garlic paste
2.5ml - ½tsp paprika
2.5ml - ½tsp cardammon pods
2 fresh red chillies, deseeded and chopped
5ml - 1tsp ginger paste
225g - 8oz baby carrots, sliced lenghthways
225g - 8oz small turnips quartered
225g - 8oz marrow or other vegetable
450g - 1lb pre cooked couscous
15ml - 3tsp olive oil
225g - 8oz courgettes sliced lengthways
225g - 8oz broad beans
4 tomatoes quartered
1 large bunch coriander
1 bunch parsley chopped finely
55g - 2oz butter
salt and pepper for taste

Method

In a saucepan put the washed and cut lamb with 900ml -1½ pints of water. Add the onion, garlic, spices and seasoning. Bring to the boil and cover with a tight fitting lid. Simmer gently for about 30 minutes. Add the vegetables and cover again simmering. In a large bowl pour about 300ml - ½ pint of water and stir well. Leave for 10 minutes and again add the same amount of water and the oil and with a fork make sure the grains are separated. Leave for a further 10 minutes until the grains have separated and are swollen. Steam over a saucepan of boiling water for another 10 minutes.
Add the tomatoes and herbs to the lamb and cook until the lamb is tender.
Turn the couscous onto a large platter and dot the butter over the top stir in and season. Form into a mound with a large well in the centre and fill it with the lamb. With a slotted spoon lift out the vegetables and decorate around the couscous and serve the remaining broth in a separate bowl.

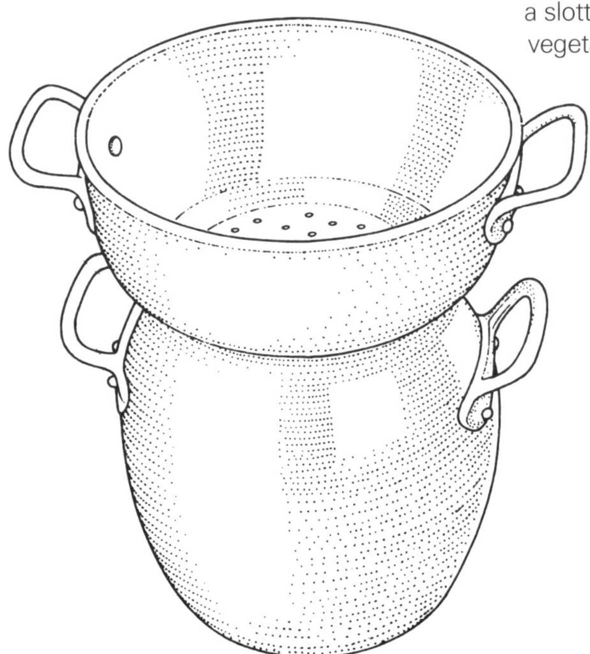

Tah Chin

While many Middle Eastern dishes have similar origins every region, every country, every town and, in days gone by, every family had its own way of preparing any single dish. Some regions have become synonymous with certain dishes.
The Persian Khoresh is especially interesting. The cuisine of this area can be traced back over two thousand years back to the time of the Parthians.
This community's diet originally consisted of millet, porridge, olives, figs, beans, cheese and milk.
Rice was a luxury grown on the northern borders of the Caspian Sea, but it gradually became more readily available. Although a wide choice is now available, nothing beats rice from Iran. Its smell, texture and flavour are unique.
No other Middle Eastern country prepares rice as the Iranians do.
Cooking rice to perfection is almost a matter of national pride.
Meat and poultry are valued for their protein content but dried beans or vegetables are substituted if meat is not used.
Tah chin (Tah cheen) is similar to biryani though it has a truly unique flavour, fragrance and appearance.
The dish is easy to prepare but common sense and creativity will do it full justice.

Ingredients

1 medium chicken cut into pieces
800g - 1lb 12oz rice
450g - 1lb plain yoghurt
1 onion
salt & pepper to taste
2 egg yolks
5ml - 1tsp ground saffron
75ml - 5tbsp chicken stock
5ml - 1tsp cumin powder
sunflower oil

Method

Wash the chicken. Cook it in a small amount of water with a little salt and pepper and a whole onion for about 30 minutes.
Discard the onion when the chicken is cooked. Take out the chicken, place on a plate and allow to cool.
In a bowl, mix the yoghurt, egg yolks, salt and pepper, cumin, saffron and chicken stock.
This mixture should be fairly liquid. Marinate the chicken in this overnight or for a few hours in the fridge.
The next day boil water in a large pan with 5tsp salt. Add the rice which has been pre-soaked.
Boil the rice for about 10 minutes until almost cooked. Drain. Pour a few tablespoons of cold water over the top to refresh the rice and drain again thoroughly.
Lift out the chicken pieces. Thoroughly mix quarter to half of the rice with the extra marinade until the rice has absorbed the liquid and has coloured yellow.
Pour enough oil into a heavy pan to cover the bottom. When the oil is quite hot add the yellow rice. Cover the base of the pan to make a layer.
Arrange the chicken pieces over this and cover with the remaining white rice.
Cover the pan with a lid and cook on medium heat for 5 minutes. Then remove the lid and wrap a kitchen towel around it.
Replace it firmly on the pan and reduce the heat to its lowest setting. Let the pilau cook for an hour.
When serving turn the dish out on to a tray - like a cake - to reveal the mouth-watering crispy golden pilau.
Vegetarians can replace the meat content with quorn which is available from large supermarkets.

Javanese Potatoes with Tamarind Sauce

This dish from Java is traditionally served with other Indonesian or South East Asian dishes, and even with chicken or meat.

Ingredients

4 medium sized potatoes
1 medium onion chopped
5ml - 1tsp garlic paste
½ red and ½ green chopped peppers
30ml - 2tbsp peanut oil/or vegetable oil
125ml - 4 fl oz tamarind water
15ml - 1tbsp muscavado sugar
coarse salt
oil for deep frying
coriander or parsley leaves

Method

In the oil fry the garlic, peppers and onion until soft. Add the tamarind water dark brown sugar and salt and mix well. Bring to the boil and simmer until the liquid has been reduced to a thickish paste.
Cut the potatoes into thin slices and fry until golden brown.
Combine with the sauce and serve with a sprinkling of coriander or parsley leaves.

Indonesian Spiced Mackeral

Indonesians traditionally serve this dish with with plain white rice or with grilled tomatoes

Ingredients

4 small mackerals, cleaned and washed
15ml - 1tbsp vinegar
1 medium onion chopped
185ml - 6 fl oz water
60ml - 4tbsp fresh green chillies pulverised into a paste with juice of ½ fresh lime
30ml - 2tbsp garlic paste
coarse salt and freshly ground pepper to taste
45ml - 3tbsp peanut oil

Method

Smear the fish insides with a little vinegar and oil and grill. Meanwhile combine the onion water, chilli garlic in a blender and puree.
Heat the oil in frying pan and fry the mixture over a medium heat. Correct the seasoning as required and when the fish is cooked, spoon the hot mixture over the fish. Serve immediately with a sprig of parsley.

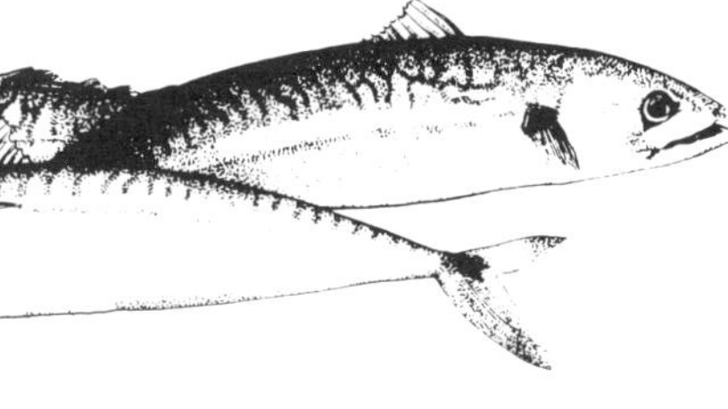

Malai Chicken

The combination of saffron and yoghurt and cream make this dish different then the rest.

Ingredients

480ml yoghurt
250ml - 9 fl oz single cream
175g - 6oz melted butter
2 medium onions skinned and left whole
10ml - 2tsp chilli powder
5ml - 1tsp turmeric
45ml - 3tbsp garlic paste
45ml - 3tbsp ground almonds
saffron strands soaked in warm milk
6 chicken breasts
salt to taste

Method

Boil onions in water until soft. Drain and blend in a food processor with the yoghurt, cream, butter, salt, turmeric chilli powder, garlic and almonds. Grease an oven proof casserole dish and place the breasts in the bottom pour the paste over and mix well. Leave to marinate in a cool place for a couple of hours.
Pre heat the oven to gas Mark 4 (180°C/350F). Cover with foil and a tight fitting lid bake for 40 minutes until the chicken is cooked and the butter should have risen to the top. Just before serving add the saffron to the meat and stir in gently, serve hot with rice.

Chicken & Macaroni Balls

Asian cookery offers an almost endless supply of savoury snacks. Some are heavy, while others are lighter on the stomach. Most savouries are suitable as starters, elevenses or even to serve with beverages and contrasting deserts. They are no rules as such or formalities for the exact time when they can be served. Savouries are welcome at any time and todays recipe, chicken and macaroni balls, is not truly Asian. The spices may be but the macaroni is most certainly Italian. The green chillies provide a bridge between the two types of cuisine, adding greatly to the taste.

Ingredients

450g - 1lb chicken breast cubes
2 tins macaroni and cheese
8 green chillies
10ml - 2tsp garlic paste and salt to taste
115g - 4oz cheddar cheese grated
5ml - 1tsp coriander powder
½ bunch chopped coriander
5ml - 1tsp dark soy sauce
breadcrumbs
1 beaten egg
plain flour as necessary

Method

Wash and drain the chicken cubes. Mix all the ingredients together accept the egg, breadcrumbs and plain flour. Mix well. Add sifted flour, enough to make the mixture like a soft dough. With your hands form into roughly shaped balls, coat with plain flour, dip into beaten egg and finally roll into breadcrumbs. Fry on medium heat in hot oil. Drain well and serve hot with chutney.

Kashmiri Lamb Chops

Kashmiri lamb chops are cooked in a unique way, firstly being boiled in milk then smeared with masala and fried. Despite the many spices used to flavour the meat, this dish actually has a very mild taste, and makes a delicious starter or even part of a main meal served with rice flour rotla or chappattis.

Ingredients

10/12 lamb chops
1 bayleaf
2.5ml - ½tsp fennel seeds
2.5ml - ½tsp black peppercorns
2 green cardommon pods
7.5ml - 1½tsp salt
30ml - 2tbsp plain flour
10ml - 2tsp chilli powder
10ml - 2tsp garam masala
5ml - 1tsp garlic paste
5ml - 1tsp ginger paste
oil for frying
450ml - 16 fl oz milk
160ml - 5.5 fl oz evaporated milk
160ml - 5.5 fl oz yoghurt

Method

Trim the chops, wash and drain well. Place in a large saucepan with the fennel seeds, peppercorns, cardommon, salt, bayleaf and milk. Boil on high heat. When the mixture has started boiling rapidly, lower the heat and simmer until the milk has been reduced to half the original volume.
Add evaporated milk and continue cooking until the meat is tender and almost all the liquid has reduced.
Meanwhile, blend together the yoghurt, chilli, flour, ginger/garlic, garam masala and the salt.
Discard the whole spices and add the chops to the spicy yoghurt mixture.
Heat the oil in a wok and fry the chops until they are golden brown on both sides. Serve hot with slices of lime.

Vegetarian Tajine

Moroccan cookery offers many imaginative and tasty dishes that vary considerably from one region to another.
The ingredients may not change greatly but the methods and customs do, with each cook striving to preserve originality.
Moroccans enjoy entertaining foreigners. They are famed for their generosity and for the magnificence of their tables. Lavish and visually exciting food stimulates the appetite the very moment it is brought into the room. A large decorative serving dish, with colours that enhance the food, is always used. In Moroccan cuisine the presentation of a dish is extremely important. Meat and vegetables are artistically arranged, their colours heightened with spices, olives, sweet peppers and dried fruits. The spices help create a warm atmosphere. The Moroccan tajine is a round earthenware pot with a glazed lid shaped like a coolie's hat. It is used to cook stews. In North Africa tajines are cooked over coals. However, they can also be put in an oven or on a hob.
To prevent cracking the earthenware pots are seasoned before use for the fist time. To do this, half fill the pot with cold water and also splash it with water. Bring slowly to the boil and leave to boil until all the liquid has evaporated.
Clay pots are best for cooking processes that are long and slow. Gently simmered food imparts a succulent and special flavour. Tajines are available from specialist shops.
Tin-lined copper pots are also popular as they have heat-retaining properties. However, enamelled cast-ironware offers a cheaper alternative.

Ingredients

45ml - 3tbsp olive oil
2 small carrots, sliced
2 small onions, chopped
3 cloves garlic, chopped
1 green pepper, sliced
2 thickly sliced courgettes
5ml - 1tsp coriander powder
115g - 4oz mange-tout
115g - 4oz baby sweet corn
3 tomatoes, chopped
salt & pepper
juice of one lemon
30ml - 2tbsp chopped parsley or coriander to garnish
15ml - 1tbsp freshly pounded garlic

Method

Heat the oil in a pan or in the tajine pot. Fry the carrots until browned and then remove. Fry the onions until softened. Add the garlic paste and stir. Then add the pepper, courgettes and baby corn. Cook until tender.
Stir in the spices and cook until fragrant. Then add all the remaining ingredients except the parsley or coriander.
Cover and simmer for almost 30 minutes until all the vegetables are cooked. Stir in the lemon juice and sprinkle the fresh green herbs.
This dish is usually served with couscous or rice.

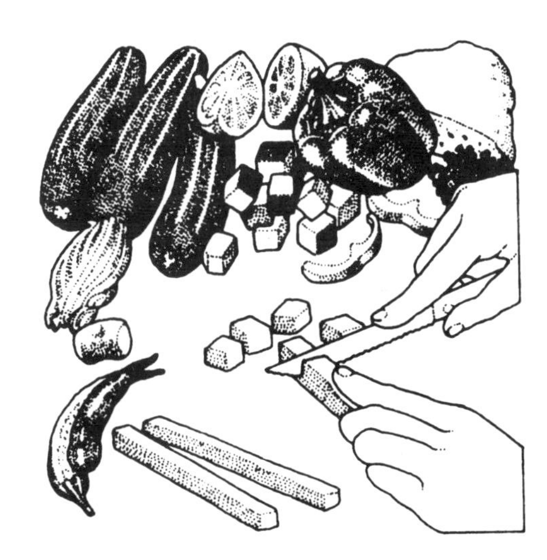

Meat Balls & Corn on the Cob Tajine

The tajine, an earthenware pot used for cooking, appears on every Moroccan menu.
The word tajine means stew but this it is only a general description of the use of the clay pot.
The tajine is usually left for hours to simmer on slow heat. Any number of recipes can be described as being tajine. Dishes of this type allow cooks free rein to use their imagination and take advantage of whatever ingredients are available. Touajen (the plural for tajine) are cooked for all seasons, any climate and every mood.
This type of cooking is best without any inhibitions over seasoning. Audacity is the key to successful cooking. As a result these dishes have a character and appearance that is difficult to appreciate merely in writing. Experimenting with and tasting different recipes is the only way to find out how well sugar goes with spices or how well corn on the cob complements meat. These ingredients may seem unlikely allies but you must trust yourself and be adventurous.

Ingredients

225g - 8oz lamb or chicken mince (mixed together with 4 green pounded chillies, salt to taste,
15ml - 1tbsp ginger paste
5ml - 1tsp garlic paste
15ml - 1tbsp coriander powde,
½ bunch washed and chopped fresh coriander
2.5ml - ½tsp turmeric
2 onions, sliced
225g - 8oz sliced mixed coloured peppers
1 tin chopped tomatoes (with
15ml - 1tbsp salt
15ml - 1tbsp red chillies
2.5ml - ½tsp garlic
2 red potatoes, peeled and chopped
2 corn on the cob, cut into 2.5cm - 1 inch pieces
2 baby aubergines, washed and chopped
45ml - 3tbsp olive oil
lemon juice
fresh coriander

Method

Heat the oil. Add onions and fry slowly until softened. Add the tomatoes with spices. Stir for a few minutes then add all the chopped vegetables. Make round balls with the meat mixture and add to the pot. After stirring the vegetables pour in 125ml - 4 fl oz of water and half of the freshly squeezed lemon juice. Place the lid and simmer very gently until most of the water has evaporated. The meat balls should be cooked and the vegetables tender. Sprinkle with fresh, very finely chopped coriander. Serve with naan breads.

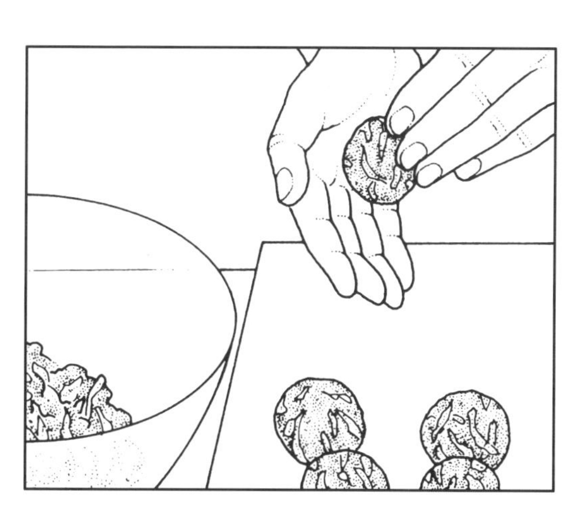

Chayote & Dhal

It does not matter whether chayote are smooth or whiskered with little spines, whether they are white or spring green in colour- they are all cooked in the same way. Usually pear-shaped with a single round flat seed, the chayote is also known as chocho or tropical squash. It is widely available from West Indian supermarkets. Originating from Mexico, the vegetable pear is grown in most hot countries. The flesh is cooked as a vegetable and its taste similar to a marrow or courgette. In this recipe I have teamed it with lentils- chana dhal, the Indian version of yellow split peas but with a better texture and a very nutty flavour. Available hulled and split, it may be cooked by itself or with rice, vegetables or meat.

Ingredients

175g - 6oz chana dhal
2 medium sized onions, finely chopped
2.5ml - ½tsp turmeric
4 green chillies
2 tomatoes
50ml - 2 fl oz cooking oil
juice of ½ lemon
1 chayote, peeled and cubed
5ml - 1tsp chilli powder
5ml - 1tsp coriander powder
2.5ml - ½tsp cumin powder
5ml - 1tsp ginger paste
5ml - 1tsp garlic paste

Vagaar Ingredients

5ml - 1tsp garam masala
2.5ml - ½tsp cumin seeds
few slices fresh ginger
15ml - 1tbsp oil
salt to taste
a few sprigs fresh coriander for garnish

Method

Soak dhal overnight. Heat oil and fry onions until they are a light golden colour.
Add all the spices except the vagaar ingredients. Braise for a few seconds.
Add finely chopped tomatoes. Slit the green chillies and sauté for a few minutes.
Then add the pre-soaked and washed dhal. Braise slowly. Add 225g - 8 fl oz of water, cover with a lid and simmer. Meanwhile, peel and cube the vegetable. When the dhal is nearly cooked, add the vegetable and more water if necessary.
Just before serving, prepare the vagaar by heating 15ml - 1tbsp oil and braise the cumin seeds, ginger and garam masala in this.
Braise for a minute then pour over the curry. Finally, add the chopped coriander.

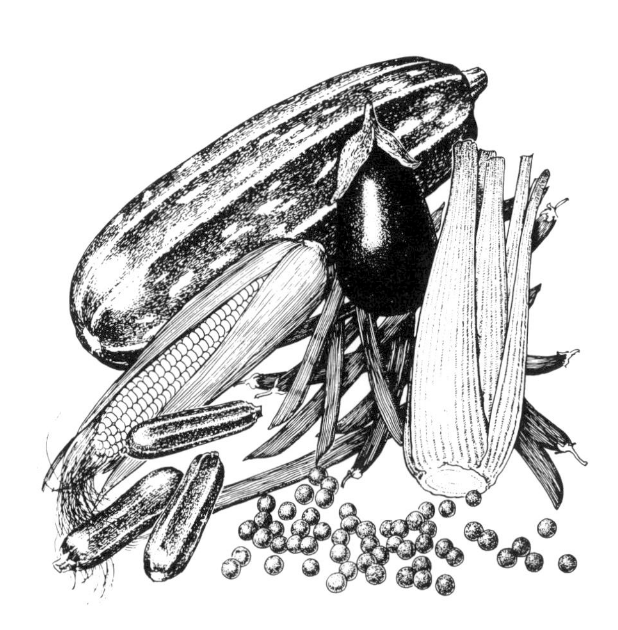

Tajine

Selection of Chutneys & Pickles

Mango Chutney

Different chutneys usually share a standard method of preparation and they are made either with fruit or vegetables. All the fruits and vegetables are finely chopped or minced. An electric mincer is useful for tougher ingredients like dates or figs.
Dried fruits may be softened by soaking in vinegar for up to 12 hours in advance before the preparation of the fresh ingredients.
In simple chutney recipes all the ingredients are usually put together in a saucepan, brought to the boil and gently simmered. But recipes can vary slightly.
Sugar produces a dense colour when cooked for a long time. If a paler shade of chutney is preferred, white sugar is added when the rest of the ingredients have cooled down.
A chutney only needs to be stirred every ten minutes. Although towards the end of the cooking time, as the chutney thickens, it may need to be stirred more frequently to prevent sticking.
Chutneys improve and mellow with time so they should be left for at least a month in a cool dark cupboard.
This recipe is a very dark and rich fruit chutney that maintains the quality of fresh mango.

Ingredients

3 under-ripe mangoes
5ml - 1tsp salt
25g - 1oz tamarind pods
115g - 4oz dried raisins (soaked for 6 hours)
slightly less than 450ml - ¾pt malt vinegar
25g - 1oz fresh ginger root, peeled and grated
2 fresh red or green chilli peppers (cored, seeded and finely chopped)
1 clove garlic, crushed
175g - 6oz dark muscovado sugar

Method

Peel and dice the mangoes. Put them in a bowl and mix in the salt, leave for an hour. Do not drain.
Put the tamarind in a bowl, pour in 45ml - 3tbsp of boiling water and leave for 15 minutes. Rub through a sieve.
Put the raisins in a pan, pour in the vinegar and add the mangoes, the tamarind pulp, ginger, chilli, garlic and sugar. Bring to the boil and simmer for 30 minutes until thick. The mango should be tender yet still in shape.
Spoon the hot chutney into warm, sterilised jars and seal immediately. Leave for 2 weeks before opening.

Pepper & Apple Chutney

Chutneys can be very distinctive with a smooth and mellow taste. They lend themselves to creative combinations of experimentation with flavours, colours and textures, not forgetting the considerable zest they add to a meal.
Chutneys can be made from a combination of fruit and vegetables with vinegar, sugar and spices.
Ideally, they should to mature in a cool, dark place for a couple of months before eating. Because the ingredients used in making a chutney very often depend on their availability at the time of making, there are no 'classic' recipes.

Chutney-making is a very personal thing. You can learn the basic method, then follow your instincts.
It is simply a matter of personal taste- some chutneys are hot and spicy while others are mild and sweet.
Careful balancing of the spices is necessary to obtain just the right mix.

Ingredients

Red, yellow and green peppers- one of each colour
225g - 8oz ripe tomatoes
175g - 6oz onions
225g - 8oz cooking apples
115g - 4oz demerara sugar
2.5ml - ½tsp crushed mustard seeds
2.5ml - ½tsp allspice
2.5ml - ½tsp crushed peppercorns
½ pint malt vinegar

Method

De-seed and finely chop or process the peppers. Remove the onions and tomato skins and roughly chop and process with the peeled, cored and chopped apples.
Place the spices in a muslin bag and simmer all the ingredients for at least 45 minutes until there is no visible vinegar.
Remove the muslin bag.
Draw a spoon across the top. The track should be clear of free vinegar.
Pour into jars and seal immediately.

Green Apple Achar

Ingredients

175g - 6oz green cooking apples
55g - 2oz fresh green chillies
22.5ml - 1½tbsp fenugreek seeds
2.5ml - ½tsp fennel seeds
45ml - 3tbsp vegetable oil
5ml - 1tsp fresh garlic paste
2.5ml - ½tsp salt
2.5ml - ½tsp garam masala
2.5ml - ½tsp cumin seeds
5ml - 1tsp dried red chillies
2.5ml - ½tsp turmeric
60ml - 4tbsp white vinegar
15ml - 1tbsp lemon juice

Method

Core and dice the apples into 1 inch cubes.
Slice the green chillies lengthways into two. Grind the seeds in a grinder until coarse.
Heat the oil in a large pan and fry the garlic. Cook uncovered on medium heat for 2 minutes or until the garlic just begins to brown lightly. Add the ground seeds and vinegar and lemon juice and remaining ingredients stir well. Cook for a further 2 minutes.
Add the apples and green chillies stir and cook until the apples are cooked but have retained their firmness. Cool and store in the refrigerator in a glass container.

Mango Achar

The art of pickling is usually learnt in the home. Many families pride themselves on their well stocked shelves crammed with rows of jars packed with almost every conceivable vegetable immersed in pickling liquid. Middle Eastern pickles are much milder than Western ones because of the dilution of the vinegar with water. Herbs such as dill, garlic and hot chilli peppers can be added for extra flavour. Indian cuisine too values contrasting accompaniments. Indeed, India is probably the greatest country in the world for making such good use of the endless varieties. Indian pickles are very spicy with some degree of heat. They range in taste from sweet to sour. Garlic, lime and mangoes are other commonly available ingredients used. The preparation often involves lengthy marinating in spices and salt. For some pickles no other ingredients are added. Some are just covered in brine, others in oil. This recipe is one of the most popular varieties of pickles.

Ingredients

225g - 8oz raw green mangoes
5ml - 1tsp salt
2.5ml - ½tsp turmeric
2.5ml - ½tsp crushed dried red chilli
15ml - 1tbsp mustard seeds
15ml - 1tbsp cumin seeds
50ml - 2 fl oz corn oil
45ml - 3tbsp fresh lemon or lime juice
karipulya leaves
½ clove garlic, peeled and chopped

Method

Wash, peel and cube the mangoes into bite-size pieces.
Add salt, turmeric, cumin seeds and chilli powder.
Mix well.
Transfer to a dish and keep in the sun or natural light for 10 days, mixing gently with a spoon each day.
Heat the oil in a pan, add garlic and karipulya leaves until they turn a golden brown.
Remove from the heat and cool completely. Add juice of lemon or lime.
Spoon the mango cubes into a jar and pour the flavoured oil over it, making sure there is enough to cover the mangoes.
Stir daily for another week until the mango is ready to eat. Eat within 3 to 4 weeks.

Lemon & Lime Achar

***In the Indian sub-continent the heat is often so intense and enveloping that it is essential for everyone to have in his or her own repertoire a pickle or achar recipe.
This will include a wide range of ingredients. Salt, oil, vinegar and lemon juice can all be used as a means of preserving, depending on the effect required.
These accompaniments have claimed their place in Asian gastronomy.
No table would be complete without their presence. Not only do they accompany meat and fish, but they are devised to complement vegetarian and rice dishes too.
Everyone has a favourite recipe and method.
This combination of lemons, lime and other ingredients produces a pickle which is sharp and tantalising - and surprisingly good with rich spicy dishes.***

Ingredients

6 lime/lemons or both (soaked in warm water for a few hours)
6 green chillies
15ml - 1tbsp fresh ground red chilli
22.5ml - 1½tbsp coarse salt
175ml - 6 fl oz lemon juice
few karipulya leaves

Method

Dry lemons on a clean cloth.
Cut into bite-size cube shapes.
Put into a bowl and add chillies, salt and karipulya leaves. Toss lightly.
Pack in a jar or pickling bottle and fill to the top with lemon juice.
Store for a few weeks before opening.
Boiling the lemon juice before topping up prolongs the storing period of the pickles.

Pawpaw & Onion Relish

Pawpaws are often known as papaya. There are orange and green varieties which can vary greatly in size. Some are small enough for one person to manage. These are the kind we see in our supermarkets and local corner grocers.
The pawpaw is a giant plant rather than a tree. When the fruit is formed it grows close under the tree and down the stem in a great cluster.
The fruit makes a perfect breakfast in the tropics, where you can eat beautifully cut apricot-pink slices accompanied by a wedge of lime or two.
Lime is an essential partner for pawpaw - as it is for a number of other mild tropical fruits. Pawpaws can be used in chutneys relishes or for general cooking.
To prepare the fruit, halve it and scrape out the deep grey seeds. Peel and use as required.
Although pawpaws are not as sweetly juicy as mangoes, their flesh is soft and rich. Whether ripe or not, green or yellow varieties make a good relish. This recipe is a light and fruity relish - an ideal accompaniment to meat or fish. For the most tasty results the relish should be freshly made.

Ingredients

1 ripe pawpaw
1 small onion
juice of ½ a lime
30ml - 2tbsp chopped fresh green coriander
1 green chilli (or more according to the hotness required)

Method

Halve and peel the pawpaw, scoop out and remove the tiny seeds. Finely chop the flesh and onion. Core, seed and finely chop the chilli pepper.
Put all the ingredients together in a deep bowl. Pour in the lime juice and mix well. Place in the refrigerator to chill for 30 minutes before serving.

Tomato & Green Pepper Relish

Relish is made in different ways all over the world. Many are rather like a cross between a pickle and a chutney.
Some relishes are thickened with flour or cornflour and some are mixtures of pureed raw vegetables, while others are cooked with a small amount of vinegar.
But no matter where they are from or where they are eaten, pickles, chutneys and relishes always add that little something extra special to a meal.
They compliment or improve the flavour of many main dishes - be it a plain roast, curry, kebabs, tortillas or beef burgers.
Their basic ingredients are similar and there are many different recipes. Almost every country in the world has its own characteristic recipe.
This tomato and green pepper relish is ideal for burgers and barbecues. It is a rich relish which can be served or stored in a covered container in the refrigerator for up to a fortnight.

Ingredients

4 tomatoes
60ml - 4tbsp olive oil
1 onion, finely chopped
1 clove garlic, finely chopped or processed with the onion
1 green pepper, cored, de-seeded and diced
1 small green chilli pepper
30ml - 2tbsp dark muscovado sugar
60ml - 4tbsp malt vinegar

Method

Put the tomatoes into a large bowl. Pour boiling water over them and leave for a minute or until the skin cracks. Drain and skin.
Heat the oil in a saucepan over low heat. Add onion and garlic. Cook for a couple of minutes.
Stir in the sweet and chilli pepper and cook for a further 2 minutes, stirring occasionally until they soften.
Turn the heat up to medium and add the tomatoes. Stir to heat thoroughly.
Add the dark muscovado sugar. When it is dissolved, add the vinegar and bring to the boil. Remove from heat and allow to cool completely.

Vegetable Pickles

Ingredients

115g - 4oz white radish
115g - 4oz cauliflower
115g - 4oz carrots
115g - 4oz turnips
5ml - 1tsp mustard seeds
5ml - 1tsp onion seeds
5ml - 1tsp cumin seeds
4 whole cloves
5ml - 1tsp fenugreek seeds
5ml - 1tsp fresh ginger root
10ml - 2tsp garlic paste
5ml - 1tsp turmeric
5ml - 1tsp salt
90ml - 3 fl oz malt vinegar
5ml - 1tsp red chilli powder
2.5ml - ½tsp garam masala
50ml - 2 fl oz vegetable oil

Method

Divide the cauliflower into very small florets and the turnips into small cubes. Cut the carrots and the radish into ½ inch sticks. Grind the fenugreek, cloves, onion seeds, mustard seeds and cumin seeds and grind until coarse. In a large pan heat the oil add the ginger/garlic and fry on a low heat until brown in colour. Add all the vegetables and salt and turmeric mix once and add the coarsely ground spices. Stir well add the vinegar and remaining ingredients. Simmer uncovered on a low heat for 7 minutes until the vegetables are firm and cooked.

Green Mango Chutney

Ingredients

6 green mangoes
250ml - 9 fl oz white vinegar
225g - 8oz brown sugar
225g - 8oz raisins
2 inch piece of fresh ginger
4 spring onions

Method

With a sharp knife cut the mango, chop the mango into small pieces.
Combine the vinegar sugar and raisins in a saucepan and bring to the boil. While it is boiling peel and slice the ginger into slivers and chop the spring onions, add all these ingredients to the mixture in the pan and simmer. Cover the pan and cook until thick.
Pour into a pickling glass jar and seal tightly.

Coriander & Coconut Chutney

Ingredients

1 bunch fresh coriander
2 medium onions, coarsely chopped
1 inch piece ginger chopped
1 fresh chilli or to taste
½ coconut grated
juice of one lemon
50ml - 2 fl oz water
coarse salt

Method

Trim the leaves from the coriander and put in a blender with remaining ingredients. Blend and put into a small bowl.

Harrissa - Moroccan Relish

Ingredients

4 dried red chilli peppers
2 cloves garlic peeled
15ml - 1tbsp caraway seeds
5ml - 1tsp cumin powder
5ml - 1tsp ground coriander seeds
coarse salt
olive oil

Method

Soak the peppers for an hour. Drain and cut into small pieces.
In a blender mix the peppers, garlic, caraway seeds, cumin, coriander, and salt.
Fill a jar with the mixture and cover with enough olive oil to preserve.
Store in the fridge.

Lemon Pickle

Ingredients

500g - 1lb 2oz fresh lemons, deseeded and quartered
55g - 2oz salt
15g - ½oz rock salt
15ml - 1tbsp cloves
22.5ml - 1½tbsp ajmo
30ml - 2tbsp sugar
10ml - 2tsp ground pepper
salt to taste

Method

Mix the lemons with the rest of the ingredients. Store in an airtight porcelain jar and keep the jar in the sun for a few hours each day to enable faster maturing. The pickle will be at its best in 3 weeks.

Mint & Promegrenate Relish

The sourness of the promegrenate seeds and the refreshing mint is ditinctive in this exceptionally quick and easy relish.
This can be served with a variety of meals and snacks.

Ingredients

5ml - 1tsp cumin seeds
115g - 4oz fresh mint sprigs
115g - 4oz onions
10ml - 2tsp promegrenate seeds
10ml - 2tsp salt
30ml - 2tbsp green chilli paste
10ml - 2tsp sugar
2.5ml - ½tsp concentrated tamarind paste

Method

Toast the cumin seeds in a dry pan, over a high heat, stir constantly until they turn dark brown in colour. Immediately pour the seeds out of the pan and set aside.

Wash and clean the mint leaves discarding the stalks, process together with the other ingredients until a fine paste forms.
Bottle and serve, this can be stored for upto a week in the fridge.

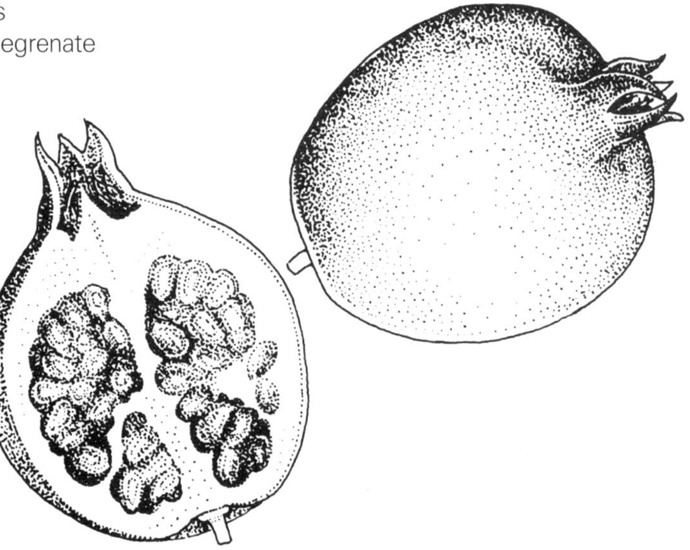

Sweet Carrot Halwa

Date Helawi

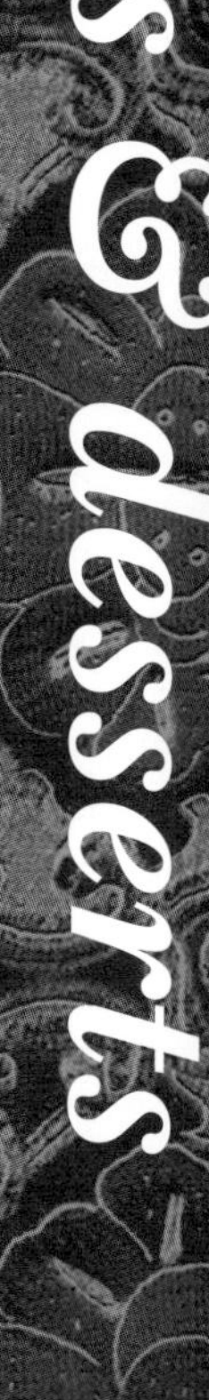

Lassi is a refreshing drink that is popular throughout India and Pakistan. In Turkey and parts of the Mediterranean the drink is known as 'ayran'.
Lassi is made from yoghurt that has been beaten smooth, mixed with water and ice and flavoured to individual tastes.
The drink can be sweet or savoury. It is sold in markets and bazaars as well as restaurants and hotels.
Lassi can be served on its own, during a meal or even after a meal. There is no better drink, especially on a hot day.
Yoghurt is made in many homes and homemade versions are generally of a better quality.
The process is simple. Making yoghurt with a yoghurt machine is easy. However, it can also be made in a wide-mouthed vacuum flask. Simply rinse the flask with hot water. Stir one tablespoon of yoghurt with 725ml - 24 fl oz of luke warm milk. Pour into the hot flask. Cover and leave for five hours. When the yoghurt has set, store in a refrigerator.
Lassi is a healthy drink that is amazingly low in calories. It is excellent for the complexion. The drink has long been recognised as an essential part of a balanced diet. Lassi is delicious, nutritious and easily digested. It is an extremely versatile derivative of milk. The drink is an excellent accompaniment to hot dishes because it helps the body digest spicy foods.
Drink once and you will be hooked. In hot weather nothing quenches your thirst quite like lassi.
Sweet or savoury, try the following recipes and experiment with other flavours, fruits and spices- the options are almost endless.

Sweet Lassi

Ingredients

600ml - 1pt yoghurt
600ml - 1pt cold water
5ml - 1tsp rosewater
20ml - 4tsp caster sugar
4 cardammon pods (discard the pods and grind finely)
15ml - 1tbsp pistachio nuts

Method

Whisk the yoghurt and water together until smooth. Stir in the rosewater, sugar and cardammon. Mix well. Chop the pistachio nuts finely. Pour the drink into glasses, add ice cubes and decorate with the pistachios.

Savoury Lassi

Ingredients

600ml - 1pt yoghurt
600ml - 1pt cold water
1.25ml - ¼tsp sugar
1.25ml - ¼tsp salt
1.25ml - ¼tsp cumin powder
fresh mint for garnish

Method

Whisk the yoghurt and water until very smooth. Blend in the salt, sugar and cumin. Serve with ice cubes and decorate with chopped mint.

Strawberry Lassi

Ingredients

120ml - 8tbsp low fat yoghurt
120ml - 8tbsp cold water
350g - 12oz fresh strawberries
175g - 6oz caster sugar
ice cubes as required

Method

Put all ingredients into a blender and blend for a few minutes. Pour into glasses and add ice cubes. As an alternative try mango slices or fresh or tinned peaches.

Melon & Ginger Lassi

Ingredients

225g - 8oz yoghurt
flesh of one melon
7.5ml - 1½tsp ground ginger
120ml - 8tbsp caster sugar (adjust to taste)
225g - 8oz cold water
ice cubes as required

Method

Blend all ingredients together (except ice cubes) until the mixture is frothy. Pour into glasses and top with the ice cubes.

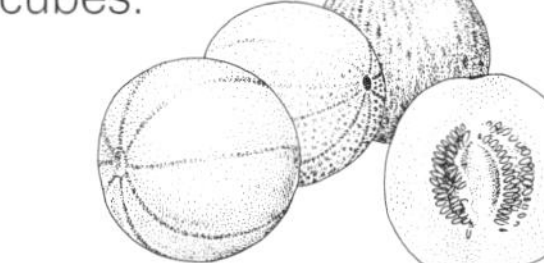
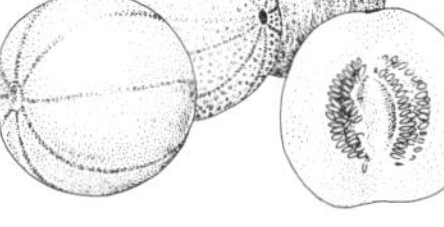

Kulfi - Indian Ice-Cream

Ice cream - a Chinese invention - was introduced by Arabs and Persians to the Middle East. Marco Polo brought the dessert to Italy in the 13th century.
Hand cranked churning pails to make the sweet at home using a freezing mixture of ice and salt became popular after the turn of this century in Europe and the Commonwealth.
However, long before all this happened, a frozen dessert was developed in Delhi, either brought to the country by the Moghuls from Kabul or originated by them in India. This was kulfi, which derived its name from the conical metal device in which it was made. Manuscripts of the sixteenth century describe the preparation of kulfi in Emperor Akbar's royal kitchen as freezing a mixture of milk solids, pistachio nuts and saffron essence in conical metal receptacles and sealing the contents.
Kulfi has been made and sold on the streets of every major city in India for centuries.
It is firmer than conventional ice cream and is usually set in small aluminium cone-shaped moulds. However, today, plastic ice cream tubs can be used instead.
Try the following recipes but be adventurous by substituting one fruit for another, creating your own formulas and flavours.
An abundance of fruit is available to give a wide range of tastes.
The fruit should always be pulverised in a liquidiser. A little should be saved for decoration.

Pistachio & Almond Kulfi

Ingredients

150ml - 5 fl oz fresh milk
30ml - 2tbsp ground rice
15ml - 1tbsp ground almonds
450g - 16oz tin evaporated milk
5ml - 1tsp ground cardammon
55g - 2oz sugar
425ml - 15 fl oz double cream
15ml - 1tbsp rosewater or 6 drops of any other flavour such as vanilla, almond, etc.
25g - 1oz unsalted pistachio nuts, shelled and lightly crushed

Method

Heat the milk until it is luke-warm. Mix the ground rice and almonds into a bowl. Gradually add the warmed milk a little at a time, making a thin paste of pouring consistency. Make sure there are no lumps.
Heat the evaporated milk to boiling point and add the ground cardammon. Take the pan off the heat and gradually add the almond and rice mixture, stirring continuously. Add the sugar and cream. Place the pan over medium heat. Work the mixture for about 15 minutes, stirring all the time.
Remove the pan from the heat and allow to cool slightly. Add the flavouring and half of the pistachio nuts. Mix well. Allow the mixture to cool completely, stirring frequently to prevent froth forming.
Pack into ice cream tubs or individual moulds. Top with the remaining pistachio nuts and freeze.
Allow to defrost slightly in the refrigerator before serving.

Mango Kulfi

Ingredients

15ml - 1tbsp custard powder
45ml - 3tbsp caster sugar
425ml - ¾ pint milk
2 medium mangoes, peeled and pureed or a 15oz can of mango pulp
150ml - ¼ pint of double cream, lightly whipped
mango slices for decoration

Method

Make a custard with the powder, sugar and milk, taking care not to leave any lumps.
Bring to the boil and let the mixture thicken. Remove from the heat and immediately place in a bowl of cold water, stirring continuously.
Let the mixture cool down completely but do not allow a skin to form. When cold, fold in the mango pulp or puree and the double cream. Pour into a suitable container and freeze.
Take out every 20 minutes and whisk vigorously to prevent crystals forming in the mixture. Repeat this 5 to 6 times.
Before serving, allow the kulfi 10-15 minutes in the refrigerator to soften it slightly. Decorate with mango slices.

Home Made Ice Cream

This recipe is certainly worth trying. It can be made with almost no effort as the food processor takes care of that, the varieties and flavours are endless. Home made ice cream is certainly more creamier and delicious. Try it and experiment with different flavours.

Ingredients

300ml - ¼pt fresh thick double cream
410g - 1 tin evaporated milk
140g - 5oz sugar
175g - 6oz desiccated coconut
flavouring
vanilla essence

Method

Place the tin of evaporated milk in the freezer overnight.
In the morning in the blender pour in the double cream and blend until frothy about 5 mins.
Open the evaporated milk which is frozen and gradually scrape the milk and add a spoonful at a time while the machine is still on. Continue doing this until all the milk has been thoroughly blended.
Add the sugar and the flavouring of your choice and continue blending for another 10 minutes. Fast freeze, if possible, in plastic or tupperware containers and when frozen it is ready to eat.

Alternative flavourings

Mint essence - with a hint of green colouring
mango pulp - with a hint of orange colouring
¼ cup ground almonds and ¼ cup ground pistachio nuts
strawberry puree - with few drops red colouring delicately mixed in before freezing giving a two tone effect.

Semolina Pudding

Ingredients

450ml - 16 fl oz water
280g - 10oz white sugar
25g - 1oz pine nuts
115g - 4oz butter
115g - 4oz semolina
ground cinammon to sprinkle or crushed chocolate flake
300ml - 12oz clotted cream
juice of one lemon

Method

Boil the lemon juice water and sugar in a pan for 15 minutes.
In a large pan melt the butter and throw in the pine nuts stir, add semolina and cook on a low heat until lightly brown.
Remove from the heat and stir in the syrup return to the heat and stir well incorporating all the ingredients together.
Cook for a further 5 minutes transferring the mixture to a serving dish.
Smooth the cream over the surface and sprinkle with cinnamon or crushed chocolate flake and serve cold.

Rice Pudding

Ingredients

1.2 litres - 2pt milk
45ml - 3tbsp ground rice
15ml - 1tbsp corn flour
15ml - 1tbsp rose water
115g - 4oz ground almonds
90ml - 6tbsp sugar
grated nutmeg to sprinkle and decorate
flaked pistachio and almonds to decorate

Method

Mix the ground rice and corn flour with a little milk until it is a smooth paste.
Heat the sugar in the rest of the milk and add the rice paste, stirring continuously with a wooden spoon.
Simmer until just below boiling point taking care not to scorch the bottom.
The mixture should thicken in 15 minutes.
Add the rose water and ground almonds, and continue stirring in one direction on a low heat.
Simmer for a further 5 minutes then remove from the heat and cool slightly before pouring.
Arrange into individual dishes garnish with remaining ingredients and allow to chill for a few hours.

Steamed Caramel Pudding

The secret of good milk pudding is in the slow cooking. And care should be taken to cover the pudding well. No water should be allowed to enter the basin. The boiling should be slow and regular checks should be made on the amount of water inside the pot. The lid of the pot should also be closed tightly. Ensure the pudding is placed above the boiling water when it goes into the steamer.
A steamed caramel pudding is a traditional recipe but, by adding a few special ingredients, the dessert can be turned into something completely different.
One alternative is saffron, an aristocrat among spices. It has a subtle aroma and a golden colour, though it is considered expensive. Cardammon is a pod containing seeds, a common ingredient in Indian spice mixes. Pistachio nuts, which have been cultivated in the Mediterranean and further east for thousands of years, are green in colour. They are ideal for decoration.
Steamed puddings are a favourite within many cultures. With the addition of these exotic ingredients a mere pudding becomes a pudding with a difference!

Ingredients

4 eggs
75ml - 5tbsp sugar
900ml - 32 fl oz full cream milk
a few strands saffron
a few drops vanilla essence
ground cardammon

For the caramel

30ml - 2tbsp sugar
15ml - 1tbsp water

Method

Put the sugar and water in a saucepan, stirring on very low heat until the sugar has melted and caramelised.
Whisk the eggs, vanilla, saffron and cardammon seeds in a basin until frothy.
Add the milk and whisk thoroughly.
Pour the caramel into the basin that the pudding will be steamed in. Spread evenly.
Add the milk mixture over the caramel. The pudding is now ready to steam. Boil some water in a pot that is larger than the pudding basin. Fill only two thirds of the height of the basin. Cover the basin with either foil or a tight fitting plate. Then cover the lid of the pot tightly but allow the steam to escape. Steam gently for approximately 45 minutes or until cooked.
When cool, turn upside down on to a plate, allowing the caramel to run over the surface of the pudding.

Bread & Pineapple Pudding

The pineapple (ananas), with its magnificent crown of leaves, is the main rival of the mango for the title king of fruits.
It has graced the tables of the rich and famous in the West since its introduction into Europe from South America in the 17th century.
The name of the fruit is derived from its superficial resemblance to the pinecone, though the two have little else in common.
The pineapple is a member of a family of tropical plants, the bromeliads, of which it is the only edible species.
Today, pineapples are cultivated throughout the tropics, especially in places where the rainfall is high.
The principal exporters of pineapples are Hawaii, the Ivory Coast and Dominica.
The pineapple is an unusual fruit in that it does not ripen if removed from the bush on which it grows.
A day before the fruit matures sweet sap shoots from the roots into the pineapple, ripening it at once.
Only at this moment is the fruit ready to be picked. It is useless to buy an unripe pineapple in the hope that it will ripen if kept in a warm place.
The best way to judge the ripeness of the fruit is to smell it. If it is ripe it should give out a sweet smell.
The outer colour gives no indication of ripeness. The crown of the leaves should be glossy, not withered or dry, and a leaf plucked from the crown should come away easily.
Pineapples are at their best during the summer months of the country in which they are grown.

Ingredients

4 slices white bread
135ml - 9 tbsp sugar
4 eggs
900ml - 1½ pints milk
30ml - 2tbsp margarine
a few drops vanilla essence
a few strands saffron
55g - 2oz desiccated coconut or freshly grated coconut
55g - 2oz yellow raisins
powdered pistachio nuts
cardammon
a sprinkle of nutmeg
finely sliced almonds
1 tin of pineapple pieces or chunks cut small (or a small fresh pineapple cut into small cubes) with 15ml - 1tbsp sugar added

Method

Break the bread into tiny pieces and soak in the milk.
Beat the eggs, sugar and margarine until fluffy and add the vanilla essence.
Add the bread the egg mixture and combine well.
Add the saffron strands, the coconut and powdered ingredients.
Then add the pineapple and half the juice from the tin. Mix well.
Pour into a 5cm - 2 inch deep baking tray and decorate with the finely sliced almonds, a few raisins and desiccated coconut. Sprinkle a little of the powdered ingredients that have been left unused.
Bake in a moderate oven for almost 1½ hour or until golden brown.
Slice and serve hot or cold with fresh cream.

Sago & Fruit Pudding

Ingredients

150g - 5oz sago
600ml - 1pt milk
100g - 3oz sugar
5ml - 1tsp cardammon powder
30ml - 2tbsp ground cashew nuts
150ml - ¼pt evaporated milk

Method

Wash the measured sago, drain and allow to stand for 15 minutes.
Boil the milk and sugar together, and reduce the heat and continue to simmer for a further 5 minutes.
Remove from the heat and add the cardammon powder, nuts and evaporated milk.
Cover and allow to cool.
Add 300ml - ½pt water to the sago and bring to the boil.
Reduce the heat and continue simmering until the sago is cooked.
Take off the heat and allow to cool. When just warm add the milk mixture and cool in the fridge.
When serving add chopped pieces of soft fruit such as guavas, strawberries or even promegrenate seeds.

Coconut Diamonds

Ingredients

115g - 4oz butter
175g - 6oz semolina
50ml - 3 fl oz milk
175g - 6oz sugar
85g - 3oz dessicated coconut
55g - 2oz plain flour
5ml - 1tsp baking powder
few drops vanilla essence
15 almonds, blanched and slivered

Syrup

125ml - 5 fl oz boiling water
15ml - 1tbsp lemon juice
225g - 8oz sugar

Method

Make the syrup first by boiling the three ingredients. When thickened remove from the heat and cool.
Pre heat the oven to gas mark 5 and make the cake.
Melt the butter and mix with all ingredients into a large bowl, stir well and transfer to a shallow baking tray.
Bake for 30 minutes or until golden brown. Remove from the oven and cut with a sharp knife into diamond shapes and sprinkle some almonds on the slices.
Pour over half of the syrup and bake for 5 more minutes until the diamonds are a rich golden colour. Be careful not to scorch the almonds.
Remove from the baking tray and serve warm serving the remaining syrup over the top for a sweeter taste.
Although they are usually eaten warm they are equally delicious chilled in the fridge and will store for quite a few days.

Sweet Carrot Halwa

Ingredients

750g - 1½lb grated carrots
750ml - 1¼ pt milk
1 cinammon stick
60ml - 4tbsp ghee
60g - 2oz sugar
30g - 1oz chopped pistachio nuts
50g - chopped blanched almonds
60g - 2oz raisins
2.5ml - ½tsp crushed cardammon seeds
double heavy cream to serve

Method

In a large heavy pan put the carrots, milk and cinammon and bring to the boil. Reduce heat and simmer for 40 minutes until thickened. Stir frequently during cooking to prevent sticking and then remove the cinammon.
Heat the ghee in a non stick pan and add the mixture, stirring lightly until the carrots have a lovely sheen.
Add the sugar, nuts and raisins and the cardammon and stir well and continue cooking on low for another 5 minutes.
Equally delicious hot or cold served with cream.

Larwa

Ingredients

Batter

½kg - 1lb 2oz gram flour-sieved
5ml - 1tsp baking powder
10ml - 2tsp melted ghee
warm water
few drops orange colour
mixture of vegetable oil/ghee for frying the kari

Syrup

½ kg - 1lb 2oz granulated sugar
450ml - 16 fl oz water
orange food colouring
a generous pinch of saffron
225g - 8oz dessicated coconut
225g - 8oz sultanas
5ml - 1tsp cardammon powder
115g - 4oz slivered almonds

Method

First make the syrup with the sugar, water saffron and food colouring. Boil until medium consistency taking care not to make the syrup thick or it will give a sugary appearance.
Make the batter with warm water and all the ingredients. Push through special ladoo maker until tiny drops of batter fall out. Within seconds they should be fried and floating to the top.
Remove with a slotted jharo and collect in a large basin. Continue in this way until all the batter is used up.
Pour the warm syrup over the kari, mix well and allow to soak in the syrup. Leave for ½ hour stir and add the coconut, sultanas slivered almonds and cardommon powder. Stir well again and until the syrup is fully absorbed. Take a handful of the kari and with your hands form into a small ball firmly pressing together. Repeat this until all the mixture is used up. Store in the fridge.

Paan Mix

Chewing betal leaf or paan is a tradition that is wholly Indian. It is usually chewed after meals as a freshener or even for its acidic qualities to aid digestion. In the past maharajas placed a betal nut in the open court and asked anyone brave enough to take on a difficult task to take on to pick it up. Betal nuts are used in many supari mixtures.On their own, they are finely sliced and chewed.
The sweet variety - widely available in Indian shops - can be stored for a few months. An infusion of betal nuts boosts a weak digestive system and sluggish liver. Today's recipe, gulkhan (concentrated rose petal paste)and coconut pan mix, is a sweet concoction that is most welcome at weddings, mehendi parties or family gatherings.
There never seems to be enough. Young and old alike are extremely fond of its taste. Gulkhan is a concentrated rose petal paste.
Gulkhan and coconut paan mix is so colourful that one just can't help reaching for it time and again. The colours include the green of the paan, the pink of the syrup and the pure white of the coconut. Eid Day at the end of Ramadan and at Hajj time is a special time for the whole of the family to feast and relax together. It is the ideal time to pass around a bowl of gulkhan and coconut paan mix. This tradition takes me back to my own childhood when my late mother sat down with the ingredients and folded the pan into triangles.
It was a treat well worth waiting for. Today, the use of an electric processor, the effort needed to make the recipe is minimal.

Ingredients

1 fresh coconut, de-husked, peeled and grated finely or shredded.
115g - 4oz paan (betal leaf) shredded in a processor
60ml - 4tbsp gulkhan
30ml - 2tbsp rose syrup or more according to the sweetness required
15ml - 1tbsp katho (this brown powder is available from Asian shops)
450g - 18oz packet of mixed saumf (sugar-coated salty funnel seeds)
55g - 2oz sweet supari

Method

Shred the coconut and washed paan. Mix the gulkhan together with the rose syrup. Add all the ingredients together and mix very well. Taste for sweetness and adjust as necessary.

Guava Delight

Recent years have seen an increasing diversity of exotic fruits on sale at British markets.
When this trend began because demand was small, exotic fruits such as the guava, mango, lychee and kiwi were not available out of season. However, the situation changed rapidly when other communities discovered what they were missing out on.
As consumer interest grew, prices dropped and the fruits became more widely available. Exotic fruits are now a common sight in most supermarkets, either in the tinned or the fresh form.
The guava is a pear shaped fruit which is usually green or a ripe yellow. This fruit imparts a wonderful aroma and carries soft pips inside which are edible.
The flesh has a distinctive taste to it and tastes delicious eaten alone or as a desset. it adds a colour and taste to any dessert. Available throughout the year from countries such as Africa, India and Mexico among others.
The guava contains the highest vitamin C content then any other fruit and the contents of a tin provide 600% of the recommended daily intake of the vitamin C.
Guava Delight is a recipe collected from Southern Africa, easy to make and to enjoy.

Ingredients

170g - 6oz tin sterilised cream
1 small tub of fresh single cream
3 tins of guava halves in syrup
1 cup china grass (agar agar)
2 cups boiling water
20ml - 4tsp sugar
deep red food colouring

Method

Boil the agar agar, water, sugar and food colouring until the grass has dissolved and the setting point has been reached.
Pour out into a dish and allow to cool and set.
Meanwhile, blend together the sterilised cream, and fresh single cream, and the syrup from the guava tins until light and frothy.
De seed the guava halves and blend until soft and mushy.
Grate the agar agar which has set and mix well with the cream mixture and guava puree. Chill in the fridge before serving.

Date Helawi

The idea of working with the children in the kitchen might sound rather alarming but it can be quite enjoyable.
The conversations that take place during the cooking sessions are rather comical. It makes you wonder where children get their ideas from!
Baking and cooking are enjoyable and relaxing pastimes. Passing on these skills to your children is a valuable inheritance. And they will learn to appreciate more the time and effort put into the preparation of meals.
There are many simple yet delicious recipes which youngsters can try. They can then delight in taking the fruits of their labour to neighbours' or relatives' homes, proudly declaring: "I cooked that!"
However, it is important to supervise children at all times. Cooking on the stove should be performed by an adult.
But, as far as possible, the adults should keep in the background. This will encourage the children to read the recipe on their own and follow the simple instructions.
The following recipe requires practically no baking and very little cooking but the end result is nourishing, satisfying and absolutely delicious.
The recipe includes plenty of dates- an important food for Arabic diets, especially for people living in desert areas.
Dried dates keep for a very long time. Those which are pressed into blocks are quite hard and a bit tasteless but dates arranged in oval boxes on plastic stalks are sweeter and juicier.
Dates are produced in Israel, California, Iran, Tunisia, Algeria and Saudi Arabia. They contain 60 to 70 per cent sugar as well as vitamin A and B Complex.

Ingredients

280g - 10oz butter
280g - 10oz sugar
2 eggs
1 large packet of Rich Tea or Marie biscuits
500g 1lb 4oz dates (stoned) - packaged ones will suffice
115g - 4oz desiccated coconut

Method

Break the biscuits into rough pieces about quarter of the original size. Chop the dates very finely.
Melt the butter and sugar in a pan. Keep stirring until the sugar has dissolved and the butter is completely melted. Add the dates to this and simmer slowly until they have softened. Remove from the heat and quickly add the well-beaten eggs. Beat into the mixture. Return to the stove and add the biscuits.
Cook gently for a few minutes until the biscuits are well coated with the date mixture.
Turn out on to foil and spread thinly. Sprinkle with desiccated coconut on the roll and wrap in foil. Chill for a few hours then slice thinly with a sharp knife. The sweet is now ready to be eaten and shared.
Apart from the cooking process, the children can take part in all aspects of the preparation of this sweet.

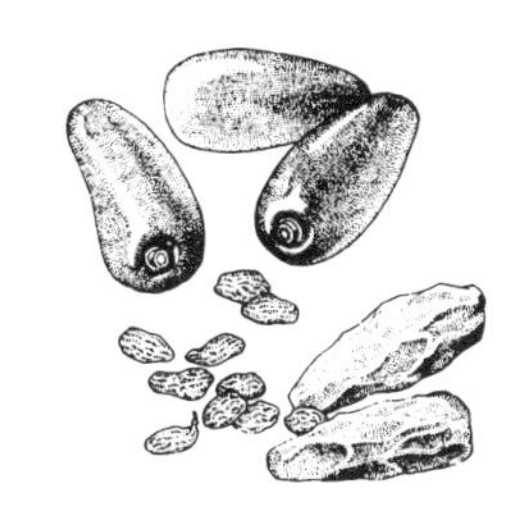

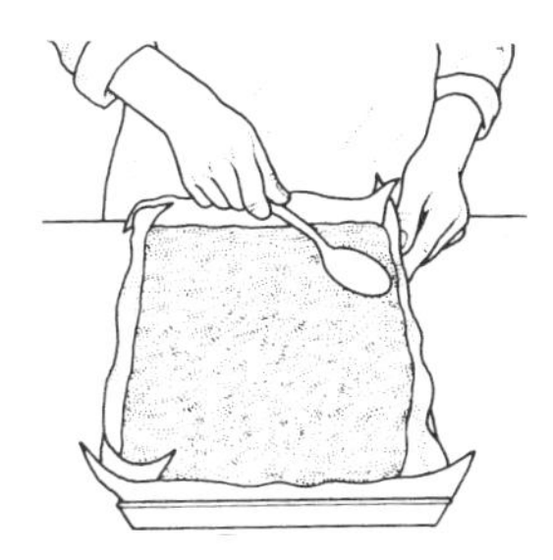

Tomato Waterlillies

With sharp knife cut zigzags through middle of tomato in 7 points. Pull apart gently.

Onion Chrysanthemums

Cut into 4 to about 1cm above the base. Continue cutting with more divisions. With fingers gently pull the petals away from the centre. Leave in bowl of iced water 20-30 minutes

Radish

Prepare as for onion chrysanthemums or cut thin petals around radish. Leave in iced water to open out.

Carrot Curls

Slice carrot paper-thin lengthwise with the aid of a potato peeler into broad strips 7-10cm long. Put a few strips together one on top of another and roll around a finger. Fasten with a cocktail stick. Place in a bowl of iced water for about an hour until crisp and curled. Remove the cocktail stick and arrange the separate curls to form a flower. Secure a cocktail stick through the centre with an olive or onion to make the flower centre. Add parsley leaves at base to form leaves.

Grapes

To skin, plunge into boiling water for 2 minutes then cold - skins come off easily. Brush with egg-white or dip bunches in lemon juice, roll in castor sugar. Dry on wire rack. Use for decoration.

Dry Fruit

To improve flavour, immerse in boiling water before use to make them swell out and appear plump.
Spread washed seedless raisins in a flat pan. Cover. Place in slow/moderate oven until wrinkles come off.

Tomato Peel Roses

Take a firm red tomato for each rose. Peel carefully around the whole with a sharp knife not breaking the peel. Wind round and round beginning with the tip opposite the stem. Wind one end of peel tightly to form the centre. Wind the rest less tightly. Fasten with a cocktail stick. Group several together on parsley or watercress.

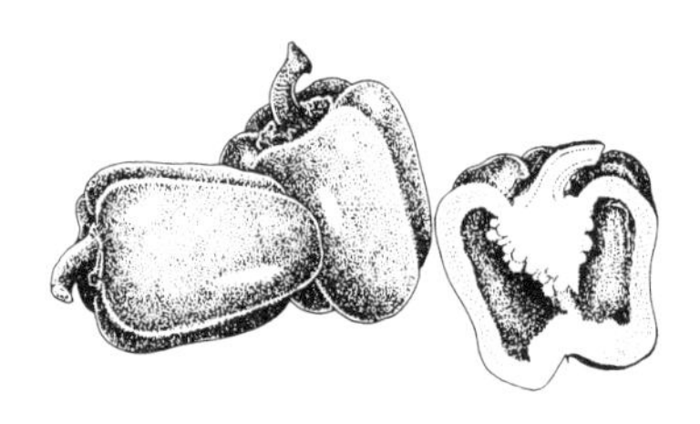

Green Peppers

Slice thinly across, remove white portions and seeds. Place in bowl of iced water to make crisp or cut rings into strips then chop into tiny pieces.

Melonball Cocktail

Using a ball-cutter fill glasses with balls of scooped out watermelon, or a combination of other fruit. Drip lemon juice over and serve chilled.

Seafood Cocktail

Combine fruit e.g. pieces of pineapple or grapefruit with cooked shrimp or flaked prawns, lobsters, etc season. Serve chilled in lettuce lined glasses or shells. Garnish with lemon or seasoned mayonnaise.

Fruit

Pierce bits of colourful fruit onto toothpick - whole strawberries, melonballs or cubes, skinned grapes, banana slices dipped in lemon juice, orange or pineapple wedges dipped in chopped parsley and so on.

Pineapple Boats Or Orange Cups

Cut in half lengthwise. Scoop out flesh with curved knife. Cut into cubes and replace with other fruit cut up garnish with mint or watercress.

Dates

Fill pitted dates with nuts such as pecan, cut-up marshmallows or candied ginger. Roll in sugar.

Potatoes

Serve Duchess Potatoes for added grandeur. Beat 2 eggs add to about 3 cups of mashed potatoes. Shape into rosettes or place mounds in a border around roasted meat or baked fish. Brush with butter, brown in hot oven.

Index